Heart Medicine Volume II

Heart Medicine
Volume II

More Devotions for Imperfect Women Based
on the Perfect Truth of God's Word

"A merry heart doeth good like a medicine: but a broken
spirit drieth the bones." Proverbs 17:22

Greta M. Brokaw
Xulon Press

Xulon Press
2301 Lucien Way #415
Maitland, FL 32751
407.339.4217
www.xulonpress.com

Scripture quotations taken from the King James Version (KJV)–*public domain.*

Printed in the United States of America.

ISBN-13: 9781545616222

Table of Contents

Are You Saved?

The first, essential dose of heart medicine is salvation through the shed blood of Jesus Christ. Be sure that you've taken these important truths to heart:

1. **Life is short.**

   "For what is your life? It is even a vapour, that appeareth for a little time, and then vanisheth away." - James 4:14b

2. **Death is sure.**

   "And as it is appointed unto men once to die, but after this the judgment." - Hebrews 9:27

3. **Sin the Cause.**

   "For all have sinned, and come short of the glory of God." - Romans 3:23

4. **Christ the cure.**
   "But God commendeth his love toward us, in that, while we were yet sinners, Christ died for us." - Romans 5:8

*"For the wages of sin is death; but the gift of God
is eternal life through Jesus Christ our Lord."*
- Romans 6:23

Pray a simple prayer.

Tell God that you know that you are a sinner and you cannot save yourself. Ask him to forgive your sins and to be your personal Savior and the Lord of your life.

That's all it takes.

If you prayed that prayer sincerely, you are forever saved (I John 5:11-13). But don't stop there! Get into the Word, get into a Bible-believing church, and get serving!

Sore Subjects

"Come, see a man, which told me all things that ever I did: is not this the Christ?" - John 4:29

"For God sent not his Son into the world to condemn the world; but that the world through him might be saved." - John 3:17

Scripture Reading: John 4:5-30

C all me crazy, but there are a few things about myself that I'd just rather not draw attention to (OK, maybe more than a few things). But if we're honest, I think we all have one or more sore subjects. Whether it's something in our current circumstances or something from our past, each of us has incidents, issues, and ongoing realities that we'd really rather forget. And we often have an official statement prepared to redirect the conversation when questions start to creep dangerously close to our sore subjects. Worried about the reactions that our sore subjects might cause (in ourselves and in others), we'll do just about anything to avoid bringing attention to them.

In John 4, the woman at the well was desperately trying to avoid any kind of attention altogether. It seems that she had already received way too much of the wrong kind of attention.

She was not the most popular girl in town (not with the w
anyway), and her notoriety forced her to practically sne.
the local watering hole, at the time of day when most won
were hiding from the heat.

When she got to the well on this particular day, she found
strange man who requested a drink of water and offered "living'
water to her. It confused her at first, but what came next completely grabbed *her* attention.

When Jesus tells the woman at the well to go and get her
husband, she gives him her official statement on this sore subject, "I have no husband." But her feeble attempt to hide the
truth reveals far more truth than she ever could have imagined.
This man knows everything. He knows the truth about her, her
past *and* her current circumstance. And yet, His kindness continues, and His offer of Living Water still stands.

In a life that is defined by her sore subjects, the compassion
of this man amazes her. He doesn't dismiss her sin condition - He
tells it like it is. But He doesn't dismiss her either. This woman
was desperately trying to avoid the condemnation of those who
knew the truth about her. She was stunned to find that Jesus knew
all of that truth and more, and yet, He was not waiting to condemn her - He was waiting to save her (John 3:17).

Forgetting the whole reason she came to the well in the first
place, she now runs to share her personal story of redemption,
"Come, see a man, which told me all things that ever I did..."

In a moment, her sore subjects were forgiven and forgotten.
She went from outcast to evangelist, and the people she had
once avoided were now the people who needed to hear the
truth about Jesus.

That's the amazing thing about an encounter with Jesus.
Your story - not your official statement, but the real story that
only God knows - suddenly takes on a whole new meaning.
Oh, don't get me wrong - "wrong" is still wrong - but when
we meet "the Lamb of God which taketh away the sins of the
world" (John 1:29), we have the incredible opportunity to be

justified by faith (Romans 5:1), forgiven (I John 1:9), and made new (II Corinthians 5:17). We find mercy and unconditional love at the foot of the cross (I John 1:7, Galatians 2:20). And we find a chance to drop our official statement and rewrite our story for the glory of God.

What are your sore subjects? Maybe they're things that you've done. Maybe they're things that others have done that you've never gotten over (I would imagine the woman at the well had both *done* wrong and had *been* wronged many times). Whether you realize it or not, whether you can even identify all of your sore subjects or not, God knows them all, and He wants to set you free from every last one of them (John 8:36).

He knows everything about you, and yet, His love for you is unconditional, and His offer of new life still stands (John 10:10, Romans 5:8, Ephesians 2:8-9). If you don't know Him, I suggest that you give His offer your full attention (you'll never regret it). And if you do know Him, then you know that this is one subject that should never be avoided.

YOUR PRESCRIPTION

Talk to God about your sore subjects. He already knows them, but He wants to give you deliverance and the "peace that passes understanding". Stop avoiding the subject and give Him the chance to finally set you free.

SELF EXAMINATION
Is God speaking to you about a problem with your heart?

_____

_____

_____

_____

_____

TREATMENT PLAN
What steps do you need to take to address your heart problem?

_____

_____

_____

_____

_____

In Sickness & In Health

*"Our soul waiteth for the Lord: he is our help
and our shield." - Psalm 33:20*

*"...Give me neither poverty nor riches; feed me
with food convenient for me: Lest I be full, and
deny thee, and say, Who is the Lord?"*
- Proverbs 30:8b-9a

Scripture Reading: II Kings 20

Hezekiah seemed to get everything right. From the time
he had taken the throne at age 25, he relied on the Lord,
and the Bible states that there was never another king like him
in Judah - a pretty powerful statement (II Kings 18).

When the Assyrian army threatened to take Jerusalem,
Hezekiah took the evil letter they had sent him and literally
laid it out before the Lord (a great plan for any problem). The
result in II Kings 19 was a miraculous victory, as the angel of
the Lord killed thousands of Assyrian soldiers in their own
camp before they ever had the opportunity to attack Jerusalem.

Every time trouble threatened, Hezekiah cried to the Lord
for help. And threaten it would, in II Kings 20, when Hezekiah
found himself on his death bed. The early verses of the chapter

paint a vivid picture, as the prophet Isaiah delivers a grim prognosis. You can almost see Hezekiah rolling over in his bed (Verse 2 says he "turned his face to the wall"), weeping and begging the Lord for mercy. Isaiah doesn't even get out of the palace before the Lord tells him that Hezekiah's life will be extended by 15 years (Verses 4-6).

The Lord also promises to continue to protect Judah from the ever-advancing Assyrians. Hezekiah can breathe again, as the Lord replaces sickness with health, and places His hand of protection over the kingdom. But as Hezekiah settles in for his final 15 years, he makes a tragic mistake.

When visitors come from Babylon, the renewed Hezekiah gives them VIP treatment and a grand tour. Without any divine guidance, Hezekiah shows his guests the full inventory of the Lord's blessings - without ever mentioning the Lord (Verses 12-13). Every last corner of his house, every last coin in his treasury, is displayed (not a brilliant move). Some say that Hezekiah's pride got the best of him. Some think he wanted an alliance with the Babylonians as more insurance against the Assyrians. Whatever his motive, he was out on a limb, seemingly forgetting that he needed God in health as much as he did in sickness.

By Verse 15, Isaiah has returned with another grim prognosis - this time for the kingdom of Judah. Everything that Hezekiah trotted out to impress the Babylonians will someday *belong* to the Babylonians, and even Hezekiah's own descendants will be carried away as slaves. It's a sad and disappointing end to a great run of faith, and Hezekiah's only comfort lies in the fact that his 15 years will be up before the prophecy comes to pass.

It's so easy to call on the Lord in times of trouble, and so easy to forget that we need Him just as much when life is good. In Proverbs 30:8-9, the writer makes reference to our tendency to ignore God in times of prosperity. We can be just like Hezekiah, showing off the rewards of our accomplishments, and forgetting that the Assyrians of life would have us for lunch, were it not for the mercies of the Lord (Lamentations 3:22-24, I Corinthians 1:30-31).

The truth of the human condition is this - our need for God is constant, consistent, and never-ending. In good times and in bad, anything we have is just a product of His grace and mercy (Deuteronomy 8:18, Ecclesiastes 3:13, James 1:17). Today may be a great day, but we all know that tomorrow can be a completely different story.

Wherever you are in the story of your life, know that you need God equally on every page and throughout every chapter (Psalm 91:14-16, 142:5). The good news is, He is the same yesterday, today and forever, and the Bible says His mercies are new every morning (I love that promise).

Whatever the day holds, I hope you know that God holds you. He loves you with an everlasting love, He has a plan for you, and He is the One whose grace sustains us - in sickness and in health.

YOUR PRESCRIPTION

*Where are you right now? Are you in a place of heartache and sickness or in a place of happiness and health? Either way, the Lord needs to hear from you right now. Praise Him that He is there for you in every season of life, and give Him glory for both the blessings you have **and** the blessings you need.*

SELF EXAMINATION
Is God speaking to you about a problem with your heart?

_____

_____

_____

_____

_____

TREATMENT PLAN
What steps do you need to take to address your heart problem?

_____

_____

_____

_____

Redefining Moment

"The Lord will perfect that which concerneth me: thy mercy, O Lord, endureth for ever: forsake not the works of thine own hands."
— *Psalm 138:8*

"Being confident of this very thing, that he which hath begun a good work in you will perform it until the day of Jesus Christ." - Philippians 1:6

Scripture Reading: Acts 4:1-21

As fishermen turned followers, Peter and John rarely got anything right during Jesus' earthly ministry. In fact, some of their blunders were downright embarrassing, while others just showed incredible immaturity and self-centeredness.

Peter's defining moments as a disciple were often marked by flashes of temper, false courage, and a mouth that was usually way ahead of his brain. When Jesus told him to walk on the water, he sank (Matthew 14:28-32). When Jesus told him to pray with Him in the garden, He fell asleep (Mark 14:33-41). He made a bloody mess (literally) when he wildly cut off a man's ear in a sad attempt to defend Jesus (John 18:10). And when Jesus told Peter that he would deny even knowing

Him, he did - no less than three times (Luke 22:31-34, 22:61). In Matthew 19:27, Peter bluntly asked Jesus what the disciples could expect in return for their having "forsaken all". And while Jesus was gracious in His answer (as He so often is with us), Peter's question showed that he still had a lot to learn about grace (Ephesians 2:8-9, II Peter 3:9).

John's defining moments are more subtle, but they reveal a heart that was just as self-serving as Peter's. In Matthew 20:20-24 and in Mark 10:35-41, John and his brother, James, approach Jesus to ask for a promotion (a move that did not win them any points with their fellow disciples). Better yet, in the Matthew account, they get their mother to do the talking for them. If you read the verses that precede their request, they've completely missed Jesus' explanation of all that He would suffer for our salvation (mocking, scourging, crucifixion), and they've skipped right on to the good stuff (heaven's throne room). John's super-competitive nature even shows up in his own gospel, where he often implies that he is Jesus' favorite (the disciple "whom Jesus loved") and emphasizes outrunning Peter on the way to the empty tomb (John 20:1-4). You have to chuckle at just how human these guys really are.

But by God's grace, in Acts 4, Peter and John just aren't themselves anymore (and that's a good thing). Fresh from spending time with the Risen Savior before His return to heaven (Acts 1), followed by Pentecost (Acts 2) and the explosive growth of the church, these two apostles boldly start preaching in the place where their message is least welcome - the Jewish temple in Jerusalem.

This is the stomping grounds of the very people who engineered Christ's crucifixion (or at least they thought they engineered it - Acts 4:26-28), and the last thing they want to hear about is Jesus' resurrection (Acts 3:13-18, 4:1-2). To top it off, Peter healed a lame man right at the temple gate, adding even more credibility to their message, and adding another 5,000 believers to the church (Verse 4).

Worried & Wanting

"The Lord is my shepherd; I shall not want. He maketh me to lie down in green pastures: He leadeth me beside the still waters. He restoreth my soul..." - Psalm 23:1-3a

"Are not two sparrows sold for a farthing? and one of them shall not fall on the ground without your Father. But the very hairs of your head are all numbered. Fear ye not therefore, ye are of more value than many sparrows."
- Matthew 10:29-31

Scripture Reading: Matthew 6:25-34

If I were a Bible character, I think I would be Martha (Luke 10:38-42). I have great intentions, but I tend to worry about all the wrong things. Martha's my girl - eager to serve the Lord, but plagued by worries, and ultimately, running in circles stressing about a whole bunch of things that don't really matter.

Although being Martha is exhausting at best, there is good news for Martha's like me. It comes in John 11, when Jesus receives word that Lazarus is ill. Verse 5 very simply says: "Now Jesus loved Martha, and her sister, and Lazarus."

Did you get that? Jesus loved Martha - worrying, whiny, wanting Martha. In moments when we are really all too aware of our own inadequacy and brokenness, it's a comfort to be reminded of the abundant love and enduring patience that God has for us. But we can still deprive ourselves of God's best for us, when we let *worry* leave us *wanting* (Psalm 23:1):

1. **Worriers miss the blessing.** Every time we run into Martha (Luke 10, John 11 and John 12), she is a tornado of activity, bent on controlling the situation, and missing out on the blessing. In Luke 10:42, Jesus' words are gentle, but crystal clear. The "better part" is the activity that centers around Jesus. Everything else, no matter how good it may be, is a distant and distracting second to the better blessing of His presence.

   This world offers endless alternatives to time with the Lord, most of them harmless, some even admirable. But that's how Satan operates. He loves to get us wrapped up in the "harmless" to hinder us from doing the stuff that really matters (Job 23:10-11, I Corinthians 9:24, Philippians 3:14).

2. **Worriers miss the big picture.** Throughout their exodus from Egypt, the Children of Israel suffered from short-term memory loss. In Exodus 15-17, they repeatedly go into murmuring mode, actually questioning God's intentions in bringing them out of Egypt (Exodus 15:24, 16:2-3, 17:2-3). The amazing thing is, Chapter 15 started with a praise service, following their miraculous crossing of the Red Sea and the watery demise of Pharaoh's army. And yet, just steps away from the water's edge, they had already lost the big picture of God's sovereignty in their situation.

   Did they really think that the God who systematically dismantled their enemies with the ten plagues could not (or would not) provide for them in the desert? We know that the Architect of the Universe had a better plan than that, and He has a plan for you and me as well (Psalm 66:5-20, 103:6-8, Jeremiah 29:11).

3. **Worriers miss the point.** In John 18, Peter takes matters (and a sword, for that matter) into his own hands. Determined to prove his bravery on the outside, but cowardly and confused on the inside, he takes a wild swipe at the men sent to arrest Jesus. He proves two things: 1.) fishermen aren't swordsmen, and 2.) he had no idea what was really going on that night. But he wasn't alone. None of the disciples were able to make sense of Jesus' crucifixion (Psalm 30:5, John 14:1-4, John 16:19-22, 32), that is, until three days later, when it became abundantly clear that the ending of their story was actually just the beginning (I Corinthians 15:1-8).

When we let worry consume us, we are just as easily blinded to God's greater purpose in our own situation. He doesn't always let us see His purpose (especially not on our timetable), but we can rest assured that He does always have one (Psalm 138:8, Isaiah 46:10, 55:11, Romans 8:28).

If you're worried about something today, I can't tell you when or how your trouble will end. Honestly, I can't even tell you that you'll come through it unscathed. What I can tell you is that there is a Savior and a Shepherd who calms fears, stills waters, and never leaves you wanting for anything that you truly need. Goodness and mercy will follow you, just as He promised (Psalm 23:6). Stick close to your Shepherd, and don't let your worries blind you to His blessings.

YOUR PRESCRIPTION

What's on your mind? If worry is consuming your thoughts today, then I highly recommend that you spend some time reading up on God's promises. Fill your head and heart with His Word, and there simply won't be any room left for worry.

SELF EXAMINATION
Is God speaking to you about a problem with your heart?

_____

_____

_____

_____

_____

TREATMENT PLAN
What steps do you need to take to address your heart problem?

_____

_____

_____

_____

_____

spies who believed God was bigger than the obstacles that they could see (Numbers 13-14, I Corinthians 3:19-20). Yet Joshua takes the counsel of his spies, instead of seeking the counsel of God (Joshua 7:2-3), sending an inadequate army (without God's blessing) and paving the way to defeat.

3. **Pride in Prosperity.** When you're on top, it's easy to start believing that you belong there (Psalm 30:6, Proverbs 2:6, 11:2, 30:8-9). Fresh from the victory at Jericho, it never occurred to Joshua that a small, unimpressive city like Ai could be his undoing (Joshua 7:4-5). But it's not our strength that stands between us and disaster - it's the Lord's (I Samuel 17:47, Lamentations 3:22, Zechariah 4:6).

In Chapter 8, Joshua and the Children of Israel experience a regrouping and a revival. After dealing with Achan's sin, they return to Ai with God's blessing and God's leading, and God provides another miraculous victory. God brings Joshua to the end of himself in Joshua 7, and then, God reiterates and renews the promises of Joshua 1 (one of my all-time favorite chapters). And after winning the victory that God intended all along, Joshua and the people return to total dependency on God and His Word.

I'll tell you what I've been telling myself for the past several weeks. Don't be afraid to come to the end of yourself (II Corinthians 12:10). Let the things that you can't control remind you to submit to *His* control (James 4:6-8). Let go, and let your failures drive you to faith. Because, when you finally come to the end of your *self*, you'll find a new beginning with Him (Isaiah 43:19).

YOUR PRESCRIPTION

If you're struggling with something today, ask God to bring you to the end of yourself. His grace is greatest when you are humbled, and you have to throw away your own wisdom, if you want to take full advantage of His.

SELF EXAMINATION
Is God speaking to you about a problem with your heart?

_____

_____

_____

_____

_____

TREATMENT PLAN
What steps do you need to take to address your heart problem?

_____

_____

_____

_____

_____

Not Fair

*"If thine enemy be hungry, give him bread to eat;
and if he be thirsty, give him water to drink: For
thou shalt heap coals of fire upon his head, and
the Lord shall reward thee."*

- Proverbs 25:21-22

*"And Joseph said unto them, Fear not: for am I
in the place of God? But as for you, ye thought
evil against me; but God meant it unto good,
to bring to pass, as it is this day, to save much
people alive." - Genesis 50:19-20*

*"Therefore being justified by faith, we have
peace with God through our Lord Jesus Christ:
By whom also we have access by faith into this
grace wherein we stand, and rejoice in hope of
the glory of God. And not only so, but we glory
in tribulations also: knowing that tribulation
worketh patience." - Roman 5:1-3*

Scripture Reading: Genesis 50

My dad always used to say to me, "Greta, your problem
is that you think life is fair." And the older I get, the
more I realize how right he was, and how wrong I am. I'll take

it one step further. I think that most of us not only expect life to be fair, but we also think that we are somehow qualified to determine what is and isn't fair (I've caught myself more than once on that one).

In Genesis 50, Joseph's infamous older brothers are in a panic. For 17 years (Genesis 47:28), Joseph's entire extended family had lived in peace and prosperity in Egypt, thanks to Joseph's mercy *and* his position as Pharaoh's right hand man.

Now, after burying their father, Jacob, the brothers are afraid that Joseph's mercy is about to run out, and the incidents of Genesis 37 (where they threw Joseph into a pit, sold him into slavery, and told their father that he was dead) are about to be avenged. Convinced that their father was the only thing that stood between them and justice (Genesis 50:15-17), they are amazed to find that Joseph defers to his **Heavenly** Father and chooses mercy (Genesis 50:19-21).

In all honesty, it's a good thing I wasn't Joseph. If I was, the stories of Genesis 37, 39 and 40 (where Joseph suffers one injustice after another, seemingly without explanation) would probably read very differently. If I was Joseph, those chapters would likely be filled with passionate protests, letter-writing campaigns, and any other form of human intervention possible - all in the name of "fairness". Mrs. Potiphar would get a piece of my mind, as would my older brothers, and I probably would not rest until I thought that all the wrongs had been righted (or at least, duly noted).

I know how my mind works when I'm not prayed up, humbled in heart, and feeding on a regular diet of scriptural truth. And it's not pretty (Romans 7:14-15, Hebrews 4:12).

It's a good thing I wasn't Joseph. It's an even better thing that I'm not God. I'm ashamed to say that, more than once, God has not lived up to *my* idea of fairness. But if I was God, fools like me wouldn't qualify for salvation. Self-righteous score-keepers like me would be unforgivable, particularly once their own scores were tallied. I would get exactly what I deserve, and

I'll tell you, it wouldn't be heaven. And yet, although there's no earthly justification, I am (thank God) wonderfully, amazingly, inexplicably justified by faith, and saved by grace (Romans 5:1-3, Ephesians 2:8-9, Colossians 3:12-15, Hebrews 9:11-12).

When you look at Joseph's story through the eyes of the world, your first impression is that Joseph would have been justified in doing just about anything to his brothers. But when you view it through God's eyes and through the lens of scripture, you quickly come to understand that none of us is justified outside of the grace of God (Romans 3:10, 3:23, I Timothy 1:15). The same evil that threw Joseph into the pit and into prison lurks in your heart and mine (Psalm 139:23-24, I Corinthians 15:56-57). And the same Savior that promised mercy to the thief on the cross is still all that stands between us and hell. The truth is, we are only justified by the blood of Jesus, and we are therefore completely UN-justified in depriving anyone else of God's mercy and grace - or our own mercy, for that matter (Matthew 5:7, 6:12, 14-15, 44-45, Luke 6:36, John 1:26-29, Ephesians 2:1-3).

God sends His rain on the just and the unjust, and in my better moments, I know that I need mercy every bit as much as those who need it from me. And by the grace of God, life is not fair, eternity is not fair, and as a result, you and I are never too far gone. Fair weather is overrated. Let mercy rain.

YOUR PRESCRIPTION

Who needs mercy? Besides you, I mean. Thank God for His mercy to you, and extend yours to those who need it. Who knows? Your mercy may be the first step in introducing them to your wonderful, merciful Savior.

SELF EXAMINATION
Is God speaking to you about a problem with your heart?

_____

_____

_____

_____

_____

TREATMENT PLAN
What steps do you need to take to address your heart problem?

_____

_____

_____

_____

_____

The Right Fix

*"For his anger endureth but a moment; in his
favour is life: weeping may endure for a night,
but joy cometh in the morning." - Psalm 30:5*

*"For I know the thoughts that I think toward you,
saith the Lord, thoughts of peace, and not of evil,
to give you an expected end." - Jeremiah 29:11*

*"But without faith it is impossible to please him:
for he that cometh to God must believe that he is,
and that he is a rewarder of them that diligently
seek him." - Hebrews 11:6*

Scripture Reading: Isaiah 30

I recently referred to my husband as "one of the few things that I got right", and I meant it. Not only is he a great husband (and the husband that God picked for me), but I truly have a ridiculously long list of other things that I have *not* gotten right. And frankly, the only reason I "got it right" when I married Paul, was because I really relied on the Lord for that decision.

But somehow, even after seeing God keep His promises in my life in so many ways, I still constantly catch myself trying to fix things (and breaking them in the process), instead of looking to Him for the right fix (Proverbs 3:5-6, Romans 7:18).

Isaiah would have understood. In Isaiah 30, he watched as the Kingdom of Judah ran to Egypt (yes, the same Egypt that had enslaved the Children of Israel some 800 years earlier) for protection from the Assyrian army.

Known for their own special brand of sadistic violence, there's no doubt that the Assyrians were a terrifying bunch. In their humanity, the people of Judah had every reason to be afraid. But Judah had something that the other victims of Assyria did not, and that was the promised protection of God. Still, they chose to repeatedly draw on the resources, the religions, and the refuge of their pagan neighbors.

It should have been so easy (Deuteronomy 30:11). Way back in Deuteronomy 28, when Moses came down from Mount Sinai, God had made His covenant with the Children of Israel crystal clear, and it was the right fix for every problem they would ever encounter. But this covenant was a two-way street. God would bless His people, as long as they truly remained HIS people.

That meant no muddying their worship with other idols and no cozying up to the cultures of the world around them. They were to worship no one but God, they were to follow no one but God, and they were to rely on no one but God (Deuteronomy 30:15-19). In return, God would protect them from their enemies and provide for them abundantly, and God alone would get the glory for their success.

And yet, after proving this covenant (the good consequences of obedience and the bad consequences of disobedience) time and time again, the people of Judah still just couldn't get it right. The chariots and horses of Egypt still looked like the best security (Psalm 20:7), pagan idols still seemed like a good bet (Isaiah 31:6-8), and a deal with Egypt still looked better than the promises of God (Isaiah 31:3).

But while they made dumb choices, and you and I make dumb choices, thank God that He never changes (Deuteronomy 31:8, Malachi 3:6, Hebrews 13:8). And incredibly, when we finally come to our senses, we need only to repent (turning away from sin and turning to God) to return to our covenant of fellowship with Him (Jeremiah 3:22, I John 1:9).

In Verse 18 of Isaiah 30, God is waiting to be gracious to Judah. It reminds me of the father in the story of the Prodigal Son waiting for his wayward son to come to his senses and return home (Luke 15:11-24). And as Judah comes to their senses, God pours out His mercy yet again. In Isaiah 30:19, He hears their cry. In Verse 21, He speaks to them and guides them once again, and as the verses progress, He blesses, restores, and defeats Assyria on their behalf.

In this life, we are constantly pressed to make decisions and take action. And this world offers endless advice on how we can fix ourselves, fix our problems, and fix the people around us. But I've learned (often the hard way) that the best decision in any situation is simply this: Fix your eyes on Jesus, and let *Him* fix the rest. He will show you what to do (Psalm 32:8, Isaiah 30:21, James 1:5). He promised.

YOUR PRESCRIPTION

What problem (or person) are you trying to fix on your own today? Stop working on your own plan of attack, and take it to Jesus instead. The only way to "make sense of it" is to come to your senses - and come to Him.

SELF EXAMINATION
Is God speaking to you about a problem with your heart?

_____

_____

_____

_____

_____

TREATMENT PLAN
What steps do you need to take to address your heart problem?

_____

_____

_____

_____

_____

Over My Head

"And it shall be, when you hear a sound of marching in the tops of the mulberry trees, then you shall go out to battle, for God has gone out before you to strike the camp of the Philistines."
- I Chronicles 14:15 (NKJV)

"Ye shall not need to fight in this battle: set yourselves, stand ye still, and see the salvation of the Lord with you." - II Chronicles 20:17a

"What shall we then say to these things? If God be for us, who can be against us? He that spared not his own Son, but delivered him up for us all, how shall he not with him also freely give us all things?" - Romans 8:31-32

Scripture Reading: I Chronicles 14:8-17

Appearances can be deceiving. I'd like to think that it at least appears as though I have it all together (and I'm probably even kidding myself there), but underneath it all, I am frequently frazzled. (Those who know me well are snickering and nodding their heads right now.) I am forever in over my

41

head, eternally struggling to hear God's still, small voice over all the other persistent noise in this world.

And yet, by God's grace, He is forever reeling me back in. Every time I start to drift off in the wrong direction, He gently pulls me back His way - sometimes with a song, sometimes through the unexpected but unmistakable guidance of a friend, and sometimes (as with this time) through a story.

God recently got my attention with a story that the Bible actually tells in two places (no accident, knowing God) - I Chronicles 14:8-17 and II Samuel 5:17-25. These passages provide identical accounts of a brief but powerful story that has provided my latest "go to" inspiration for victory in the everyday battles of life.

David was first anointed as Israel's next king when he was still a young shepherd, working on the family homestead in Bethlehem (I Samuel 16). In the following chapters, David would defeat the giant Goliath (I Samuel 17) and would go on to win the hearts of Israel and the hatred of the current King Saul (I Samuel 18:8-9).

This turn of events turned David into a fugitive, forced to flee for his life, in the face of Saul's rage. Some scholars estimate he was on the run for at least 8 years, waiting out God's timing for the demise of Saul (I Samuel 31). But while Saul had kept David on the run, Saul had not been able to keep the Philistines at bay. Having lost the Lord's blessing years before (I Samuel 15:26, 28), Saul had also lost a lot of ground to the Philistine army. Following Saul's death, David took up the task of recapturing those territories.

After reclaiming Jerusalem in II Samuel 5 (Verses 6-7), David turns his attention to the Valley of Rephaim (Verse 18), where the Philistine army has made itself right at home. He asks the Lord if He should attack, and more importantly, if the Lord will make his attack victorious (Verse 19). I love the answer God gives him.

God not only promises victory; He gives David a **signal** in II Samuel 5:24. The King James Version says, "When you hear the sound of a going in the tops of the mulberry trees..." also translated, "When you hear the sound of marching..." Either way, the picture is awesome. Imagine a heavenly host, an angelic army, marching overhead, across the treetops, and ahead of David into battle.

The second half of the verse states that God Himself will destroy the Philistines - before David even gets there. And so it goes. David is there to claim the victory for the glory for God, but it's pretty clear that God is doing all the fighting.

Maybe you're like me today, and you feel immensely over-whelmed, *under*-prepared, and in over your head in some area of your life. I encourage you to go to God, wait for His signal, and take note of what's really going on - over your head.

If you know the Lord, then know this - He is *for* you. What you are facing is no surprise to Him. He is ahead of it all. He is sovereign over it all, and He has a purpose in it. Follow Him, and He will give you the victory (Romans 8:31-39). It may not be *your* will in *your* timing, but it will be God's perfect plan for your life (Job 19:25, Psalm 37:37, 138:8, 139, Jeremiah 29:11).

Can you hear the marching? Look up, my friend. There's an army *over*head, and a victory *up* ahead. Don't give up now.

YOUR PRESCRIPTION

Give your battle to God. Follow Him into it, but let Him do the fighting. The only preparation you need is prayer, and the only weapon you need is His Word. Use them well, and wait (quietly) on Him.

SELF EXAMINATION
Is God speaking to you about a problem with your heart?

_____

_____

_____

_____

_____

TREATMENT PLAN
What steps do you need to take to address your heart problem?

_____

_____

_____

_____

_____

Choose Your Weapon

"And the three companies blew the trumpets, and brake the pitchers, and held the lamps in their left hands, and the trumpets in their right hands to blow withal: and they cried, The sword of the Lord, and of Gideon. And they stood every man in his place round about the camp; and all the host ran, and cried, and fled." – Judges 7:20-21

"For though we walk in the flesh, we do not war after the flesh: For the weapons of our warfare are not carnal, but mighty through God to the pulling down of strong holds."
– II Corinthians 10:3-4

Scripture Reading: Judges 7

Some people love conflict – but not me. I don't like what fighting brings out in me. I usually walk away from a fight, but the right fight (basically anything that threatens my family or my faith) tends to bring out a version of me that even *I* have never met before. It's not pretty, and it's usually pretty unsuccessful.

When your world is threatened, it's easy to grab whatever weapon is in reach – cruel words, careless actions, and equal and opposite reactions. Our instinct is to fight fire with fire, but God's Word cautions Christians to choose their weapons carefully - and fight fire with faith.

In Judges 7, God provided Gideon's army with some very strange weapons. After whittling their ranks down to only 300 men, God outfitted the Israelite army with trumpets, torches, and pitchers – more like props for a dinner theater than weapons of war.

By earthly standards, their advancing on the Midianite camp was a suicide mission – outnumbered and outgunned, they didn't seem to stand a chance. But just as He often does in our lives, God wanted to use the battlefield as a training ground. In Verse 2, the Lord tells Gideon outright that he has too many soldiers, because God wants to leave the Children of Israel with no doubt about *Who* actually wins this battle for them (Jeremiah 15:20, Zephaniah 3:17, Zechariah 4:6b).

It sounds like a crazy plan, but knowing that Gideon isn't really fond of conflict either (remember, the Angel of the Lord had to practically drag him out of hiding in Judges 6), the Lord gives Gideon repeated doses of reassurance.

Throughout Chapter 7, the Lord promises over and over that He will save Israel from the Midianites (Verses 2, 7 and 9). Finally, in Verses 9-15, the Lord sends Gideon on a spy mission and actually gives him a sneak peek into the mindset of the Midianites. God allows Gideon to overhear one Midianite telling another that he had a dream about them losing to Israel (a fear that had obviously spread through the camp like wildfire by Verse 9), and by the end of the chapter, that dream has come miraculously true.

Our battles are often like that. While we're scrambling for our weapons, God has already won the war. In II Corinthians 10, Paul reminds us that we usually reach for the wrong weapon. That's because we often choose to fight in our flesh. We take the one-dimensional view of our dilemma and think that we have to fight fire with fire. But (I'll say it again) God's Word encourages us to fight fire with *faith*.

I don't care how smart you are or how tough you are. On your own, you are outnumbered, outgunned, and outwitted by your true enemy (that roaring lion, Satan – I Peter 5:8). Your *enemy* is not who you think it is. Your *problem* is not what you think it is. For the Christian, every challenge to your faith and your family originates from one place – Hell. And the truth is, Hell has only one worthy opponent – Heaven. But the even greater truth is, Hell is no match for Heaven. The challenge to you and I is to see the fight for what it is and to choose our weapons wisely.

When you see the battle from God's vantage point, you'll see that Gideon's weapons weren't so crazy after all. When you're backed into a corner, remember Gideon's trumpet and sound the alarm of prayer (Philippians 4). When you're surrounded by darkness, remember Gideon's torch and let God's Word be a lamp to your feet and a light to your path (Psalm 119). And when the battle leaves you feeling weary and broken, remember that just like Gideon's pitcher, God breaks everything for a purpose. But for those who embrace His purpose, He binds up, heals, restores, and blesses (Isaiah 61).

Whatever battlefield you find yourself on, my advice to you is this – take a step back from the battle, take a deep breath, and take a moment to choose your weapon.

YOUR PRESCRIPTION

Are you in the midst of a fight right now? Take an honest inventory of the weapons that you've chosen to use. Even when you're fighting for right, that still doesn't justify using the wrong weapon. Ask God to help you to fight fire with faith.

SELF EXAMINATION

Is God speaking to you about a problem with your heart?

_____

_____

_____

_____

_____

TREATMENT PLAN

What steps do you need to take to address your heart problem?

_____

_____

_____

_____

_____

Battle-Ready

"And the brethren immediately sent away Paul and Silas by night unto Berea: who coming thither went into the synagogue of the Jews. These were more noble than those in Thessalonica, in that they received the word with all readiness of mind, and searched the scriptures daily, whether those things were so. Therefore many of them believed…" - Acts 17:10-12a

"See then that ye walk circumspectly, not as fools, but as wise. Redeeming the time, because the days are evil. Wherefore be ye not unwise, but understanding what the will of the Lord is."
- Ephesians 5:15-17

"Put on the whole armour of God, that ye may be able to stand against the wiles of the devil."
- Ephesians 6:11

Scripture Reading: Acts 17:1-14

If you like a fast-paced, action-adventure story, then the Book of Acts is just your speed. The messages and miracles are intertwined with narrow escapes, constant conflict, and a long list of bad guys.

In Acts 17, Paul and Silas are moving on from Philippi. During their time there (Acts 16), they planted a church in the house of Lydia, cast a demon out of a young woman, took a terrible beating for it, and held a jailhouse praise service that resulted in a miraculous release.

But the action is far from over. They go on to visit the synagogue in Thessalonica, where Paul will preach to the Jews (from their own scriptures) about Jesus Christ. Their reaction is mixed. Some are converted, while others are indignant and offended. The offended then become *offenders*, stirring up chaos and violence and storming the house of Jason, a local convert who has provided sanctuary for Paul and Silas.

Paul and Silas escape under cover of darkness, and continue their evangelism in the city of Berea. The reception they get in the Berean synagogue is very different. These folks don't dismiss Paul and Silas out of hand. Instead they investigate the scriptures for themselves (on a "daily" basis, according to Verse 11) and find that Paul's preaching lines up with the Old Testament.

And then the action picks up again, as the mob from Thessalonica catches up with Paul and Silas. Silas stays behind with Timothy to shore up the Berean believers, but Paul (their primary target) is forced to escape to Athens.

The Thessalonian mob came to town looking for a fight and hoping to tear down any faith that had been built up by Paul and Silas, but I submit to you that the Bereans were *battle-ready*. And here's why. While the mob wielded violence, insults, confusion, and a fierce loyalty to Jewish culture and man-made traditions, the Bereans wielded a different kind of sword - the scriptures (Psalm 119:114-116, Ephesians 6:17) - and it kept their faith strong in the midst of intense peer pressure and persecution.

Paul couldn't stay in Berea forever (and I don't believe it was God's will for him to do so). Silas and Timothy stayed for a time, but their ministries would eventually take them elsewhere as well. The Bereans needed a faith that was rooted in *personal* relationship with Christ, nurtured through personal, daily study of the scripture, and that need is as real for you and I as it was for them (I Peter 3:5).

Thank God for Bible-believing churches. Make sure you're a part of one. Thank YOU for reading Heart Medicine. Praise the Lord for fearless, truth-telling pastors and teachers, and cherish fellowship with fellow believers. *But don't stop there.* Being battle-ready means making time to be in the Bible and in prayer every day (Psalm 1, Matthew 7:24, Hebrews 4:12-16). If you're like me, most of your battles don't take place when you're in the safety and sanctuary of church. They take place in your own home, on the job, and in the world, where you're confronted with peer pressure, cultural conflicts, and the occasional angry mob.

Prepare yourself for the unforeseen battles of each day by spending time in God's Word. It doesn't have to be a lengthy time (though that certainly can't hurt). Just strive to make it sincere and consistent. I could probably review the events of the last several weeks and tell you exactly which days I failed to find time for God. How do I know? Because on those days, I failed in multiple other ways that could have been avoided if I had *started* my day with Him.

I get it. Life is hard. Days are busy. Time is a rare commodity in any woman's world. But God is faithful, and God's Word is the great antidote to all the poisons of life in a fallen world (Psalm 119:11, Isaiah 55:11). Conflict waits around every corner, but you can be a conqueror (Romans 8:31-39). Be a Berean, and be battle-ready.

YOUR PRESCRIPTION

Make the time. Start the day with God, and you'll no doubt end the day praising Him for all He did for you throughout that day. Don't be blindsided by the battles that He wants to prepare you for. Get in His Word, and get battle-ready.

SELF EXAMINATION

Is God speaking to you about a problem with your heart?

_____

_____

_____

_____

_____

TREATMENT PLAN

What steps do you need to take to address your heart problem?

_____

_____

_____

_____

Self Defeat

"Bless them that curse you, and pray for them which despitefully use you...Be ye therefore merciful, as your Father is also merciful."
- Luke 6:28, 36

"For I know that in me that is, in my flesh, dwelleth no good thing: for to will is present with me; but how to perform that which is good I find not."
- Romans 7:18

Scripture Reading: Luke 6:27-36

I think God is trying to tell me something, and frankly, I'm not sure I want to hear it. It has to do with being merciful, being humble, and doing right rather than being right. I'm sorry to say that most Heart Medicine devotions stem from the things I do *wrong*, and not the things I do right. If anything, they chronicle God's endless mercy to me, throughout my endless missteps and mistakes.

When conflict comes, it's easy to go on the defensive. And when you're sure that "right is on your side", it's even easier to move to the offensive. Sadly, our need to be right can justify a whole lot of craziness in our heads, and we can find ourselves doing and saying whatever it takes, just to prove our point.

None of that craziness is excused in Luke 6. Jesus clearly explained and clearly modeled mercy and humility. As a matter of fact, He came to earth as the human extension of the Father's mercy (Romans 5:8). That mercy had been extended in a million other ways since the beginning of time (Psalm 100:5, 106:1, Isaiah 55:7, Titus 2:11), and Christ would ultimately extend it by willingly stretching His arms out to die on the cross for millions of undeserving souls (Ephesians 2:1, 8-9) - including yours and mine.

If you break it down, everything that Jesus did in His 33 years on this earth - from His humble birth (Luke 2:7), to His itinerant ministry of mercy (Matthew 8:20), to His submission to death (Philippians 2:6-8), and His denial of any attempt to defend Himself (Isaiah 53:7) - was about *doing* right rather than *being* right. He came to do the will of His Father, not to prove Himself - not to set up a triumphant earthly kingdom as His disciples hoped - but to humbly serve the purposes of His Father's heavenly kingdom (John 4:34, 5:30, 6:38).

And think of all the people who were *clearly* wrong, who were treated with love and compassion by Jesus - the woman caught in adultery (John 8:10-11), the rich young ruler (Mark 10:21), and the crowds that would eventually cry for His crucifixion (Mark 6:34).

When we have answers and advice for everyone else, but our actions are lacking in mercy (I Corinthians 13:4-5), we may win in the moment, but I'll tell you, we're not winning on *God's* behalf. The true victories come when we fight our flesh and defeat our "self" - our self-seeking, our self-serving, and our self-defense (Romans 6:6, 12:1-2, Galatians 2:20).

Today, I want to challenge us to give up our right to *be* right. I want to challenge us to choose to have mercy for others, because we need it so much for ourselves. Proverbs 14:1 says that every wise woman builds her house, but the foolish plucks it down. Can I tell you that the real brick and mortar of any earthly home is mercy, and I wouldn't be surprised to find it mixed in with the gold that paves heaven's streets.

I'm not going to win today. I'm not going to finish my speech, or prove my point, or lay anyone out in lavender. And by God's grace, I'm going to keep all the pieces of my mind (or what's left of it, anyway) to myself. And chances are that, if I start praying like Luke 6:28 suggests, the point I was trying to make in the first place will seem a lot more pointless. I'm slowly learning that I deliver the victory to my wonderful, merciful Savior, when I put my pride aside and experience a little *self* defeat.

YOUR PRESCRIPTION

Is there a relationship or a situation where you need to humble yourself and extend mercy to someone? Remember, God's kingdom operates differently than the world – the greatest gains are made through losing, and the grandest homes are built on humility.

SELF EXAMINATION
Is God speaking to you about a problem with your heart?

_____

_____

_____

_____

_____

TREATMENT PLAN
What steps do you need to take to address your heart problem?

_____

_____

_____

_____

_____

The Weight of Words

"Death and life are in the power of the tongue: and they that love it shall eat the fruit thereof."
- Proverbs 18:21

"Now unto him that is able to do exceeding abundantly above all that we ask or think, according to the power that worketh in us, Unto him be glory in the church by Christ Jesus throughout all ages, world without end. Amen."
- Ephesians 3:20-21

Scripture Reading: Acts 9:26-28, 15:35-41

Someone recently asked me for an update on a prayer request. I was pleased to provide a good report, as I had seen God working in this situation. My friend responded with, "Well, I hope it works out, because..." What came after the "because" made my heart sink. And with just a few words, my friend casually slapped a "hopeless" label on someone that was near and dear to both of us.

Over the next few days, those words stayed with me. I tried to dismiss them. I chalked it up to a bad day, fatigue, stress, and even hormones, either on the part of my friend or maybe on my own part. But either way, I couldn't shake the feeling that my faith (and our mutual friend) had been damaged. When I finally took my hurt feelings to the Lord, I realized two things - 1) faith can be fragile, and 2) real encouragement is hard to come by.

You can't talk about real, biblical encouragement without talking about Barnabas. He was such a sincere encourager that the early church actually changed his name from Joses to Barnabas, which means "son of encouragement" (Acts 4:36-37). In a time when faith was *really* fragile and the church was just getting its footing, Barnabas shored up individual converts and whole congregations with his words of faith (Acts 13:42-44).

When the disciples had trouble believing that Paul (formerly Saul of Tarsus, who had once hunted and imprisoned Christians) was suddenly their new best friend, Barnabas stood by Paul and vouched for him (Acts 9:26-28).

Later, when Paul himself had trouble believing that young John-Mark (who would one day author the Gospel of Mark) was worth discipling (Mark had once abandoned Paul and Barnabas in the middle of a missionary journey to return home), Barnabas stood up to Paul, in favor of encouraging Mark. It came down to a parting of the ways for Paul and Barnabas, with Barnabas taking Mark to Cyprus, while Paul took Silas on his next journey (Acts 15:35-41), but Paul would eventually admit that Mark had been worth the investment (II Timothy 4:11).

We could all use a little more Barnabas in our lives - we need to *be* a Barnabas, and we need to *find* a Barnabas who will help us nurture our fragile faith with words of encouragement. But there was more to Barnabas than just kind words. Barnabas had the ability to see the God-given potential in a person.

When the disciples saw a cruel, malicious persecutor in Paul, Barnabas saw the man that God had changed on the road to Damascus (Acts 9). When Paul saw an immature and unreliable young man in John-Mark, Barnabas saw a growing Christian who could learn from his mistakes and lead others to Christ.

How did Barnabas do it? I don't think he necessarily trusted Paul or John-Mark any more than anyone else. He had seen both of these men at their worst, but I believe that Barnabas made a conscious decision to trust what *God* could do in these men (Psalm 9:9, 55:22, Proverbs 3:5-6, 30:5, II Corinthians 5:17).

The challenge for us is to take a second look at the "hard cases" in our lives - the ones who never listen, the ones who have let us down tremendously, the ones who seem as though they'll never change. Instead of viewing them through your past experiences with them, view them through your experiences with God (Psalm 34:4, 66:6-19). Then, speak *to* them, *about* them, and *in prayer* for them through the promises of God's Word (Joshua 1:9, Romans 15:13, Ephesians 3:17-21, 4:29, II Timothy 1:7, 12).

Understand that your words have weight. Be a believer in the life-changing potential of God. Be a believer in the plans and promises of God. Be an encourager, and use the weight of your words to tip the scales in the right direction.

YOUR PRESCRIPTION

Is there a seemingly hopeless situation or a person that has been on your heart? Ask God to encourage you with His promises and to help you to be a Barnabas and to find a Barnabas who can pray with you. God wants to do more than you can imagine - both in you and through you.

SELF EXAMINATION
Is God speaking to you about a problem with your heart?

_____

_____

_____

_____

_____

TREATMENT PLAN
What steps do you need to take to address your heart problem?

_____

_____

_____

_____

_____

What Is Truth?

*"Daniel answered and said, Blessed be the name
of God for ever and ever: for wisdom and might
are his: And he changeth the times and the seasons: he removeth kings, and setteth up kings:
he giveth wisdom unto the wise, and knowledge
to them that know understanding: He revealeth
the deep and secret things: he knoweth what
is in the darkness, and the light dwelleth with
him." – Daniel 2:20-22*

*"Beware lest any man spoil you through philos-
ophy and vain deceit, after the tradition of men,
after the rudiments of the world, and not after
Christ." – Colossians 2:8*

Scripture Reading: Daniel 2

If you're looking for answers in this life, you won't have
to look far. These days, there's a "spiritual" guru on every
corner, looking to peddle their own special brand of inspira-
tional philosophy. They have answers; the only question is – do
they have the *right* answers?

In Daniel 2, King Nebuchadnezzar of Babylon needed answers, and he quickly found out that his "spiritual" advisors (magicians, astrologers, and sorcerers) didn't have any. You have to give Nebuchadnezzar credit. He knew the right questions to ask. Plus, it didn't hurt that he was able to threaten his own gurus within an inch of their lives to force the truth out of them.

So what was the truth? It all started with a disturbing dream. Nebuchadnezzar woke knowing that this dream was important, but oddly enough (and providentially), he couldn't remember any of it. Enter his top team of gurus, who assure the king that they can interpret the dream, if he can just tell them what was in the dream (Isaiah 41:28-29, John 8:44).

Never known for his patience, Nebuchadnezzar is enraged and threatens to kill every last advisor in the kingdom. It's as if a light bulb has switched on over his head. After all, how *wise* can these wise men really be, if they can't even tell him what he dreamed?

Since no one has a good answer for the king, he orders the immediate execution of all of his wise men. The hit list includes Daniel and his three friends, best known as Shadrach, Meshach, and Abednego. Having recently impressed the king (Daniel 1:18-20), they are the newest recruits to the wise men team, and now they, too, qualify for execution.

Daniel immediately goes to the king and asks for time. He then gathers his three friends and spends that time in prayer (the best way to attack any problem). A vision comes in the night, and Daniel returns to the presence of the king with real God-given answers. He is able to tell Nebuchadnezzar every detail of his dream, as well as its interpretation, and he takes no credit for himself. His report to the king is saturated with praise for "the God of heaven" who reveals secrets, sets up and removes kings (a lesson that Nebuchadnezzar would eventually learn the hard way), and gives wisdom. By the time Daniel is finished, even Nebuchadnezzar admits that Daniel's God is the "Lord of kings".

Jesus said, "I am the way, the truth, and the life" (John 14:6), and, "Ye shall know the truth, and the truth shall make you free" (John 8:32). He also said, "Sanctify them through thy truth: thy word is truth" (John 17:17). It's not about picking the truth of your choice or the truth that's most comfortable for you. It's about knowing the *only* truth, Jesus, and living by the truth of God's Word.

If it's wise to know what's in your drinking water or the food you eat, then I think it's wise to know where your spiritual food comes from as well. So here's the test for any truth that anyone tries to sell you. If you can't find solid scripture to back it, don't bank on it.

Don't be fooled by clever catch-phrases and feel-good philosophy (Romans 1:25, Ephesians 5:5-13). Make sure it lines up with God's Word, and even more importantly, make sure it *depends* on God's Word (Psalm 1, II Timothy 3:16). The best preachers and Bible teachers are like the moon – they have no light of their own; they merely reflect the light of the *Son*. Humility (not popularity and showiness) is a hallmark of Christ-likeness (Matthew 7:21-23, James 4:10, I Peter 5:6), and the Bible is the only God-breathed, infallible Book there is (John 12:43, II Timothy 3:1-5, Titus 1:16).

One last lesson from Daniel – whenever you struggle to understand, pray for godly wisdom, just like Daniel did. God is faithful (Jeremiah 33:3). The truth is not that hard to find, once you know the Way, the Truth, and the Life. And He is all the truth you need.

YOUR PRESCRIPTION

Who are your most trusted advisors? Where do you go to get answers? Take an inventory and make sure that you know the Truth (Jesus), and you get your truth from His Word.

SELF EXAMINATION

Is God speaking to you about a problem with your heart?

_____

_____

_____

_____

_____

TREATMENT PLAN
What steps do you need to take to address your heart problem?

_____

_____

_____

_____

_____

Talent Show

*"When saw we thee a stranger, and took thee
in? or naked, and clothed thee? Or when saw
we thee sick, or in prison, and came unto thee?
And the King shall answer and say unto them,
Verily I say unto you, Inasmuch as ye have done
it unto one of the least of these my brethren, ye
have done it unto me." - Matthew 25:38-40*

*"Pure religion and undefiled before God and the
Father is this, To visit the fatherless and widows
in their affliction, and to keep himself unspotted
from the world." - James 1:27*

Scripture Reading: Matthew 25:14-46

Maybe I'm slower than most. OK, I *am* slower than most. To be honest, I spent years living on small eyedropper doses and select snippets of scripture. It's not that there wasn't value and truth in those little bite-size Bible servings - there certainly was (Isaiah 55:11, II Timothy 3:15-17). But over the years, I've started to appreciate looking at a verse in its context, and I find that God is always faithful to multiply my understanding, when I multiply the effort that I put into studying (Joshua 1:8, Psalm 119:124-125, II Timothy 2:15).

Most recently, I was drawn to Matthew 25. Let me paint the picture for you. Jesus knows that His time is short (Matthew 26:1-2). His disciples have only the faintest hint that something big is coming. They don't really believe that Jesus will be killed (Matthew 16:21-23), and they still don't quite understand Jesus' true purpose (to die as "the Lamb of God, which taketh away the sin of the world" - John 1:29; and to rise again - I Corinthians 15:3-5).

But in Matthew 24 and 25, Jesus is pouring oceans of truth into His disciples, knowing that they're going to need it, and that it will all fall into place for them after He is gone (John 2:22, 12:16, 15:26, 16:13). God is gracious with us that way, too - often teaching us a truth long before we know how, why, and when we will need that truth.

Now, back to Matthew 25. Jesus is telling the parable of the talents. In summary, two servants get it right - multiplying the resources entrusted to them by their master (Verses 19-23). One gets it horribly wrong, putting the talent to no use at all, and rendering himself "unprofitable" in the process (Verses 25-30).

Then in Verse 31, Jesus seems to suddenly switch gears, speaking of the Judgment Seat, where we will answer for all that we have or haven't done (II Corinthians 5:10). But of course, He isn't really switching gears at all. He talks about feeding and clothing the poor, taking in strangers, and visiting the sick and the poor (Micah 6:8, I Timothy 2:1-4, II Peter 1:7-9, 3:9, Jude 1:21-23). And after mulling it all over, I've come to a few conclusions:

1. Whatever "talents" you or I have - be they gifts, goods, money, time, or resources - are not really given to us for our benefit. They are given to us for the benefit of others and the glory of God (Proverbs 3:27, Ephesians 2:10).
2. When we seek to do God's will and to obediently distribute those "talents", God is able to entrust us with more of His Kingdom work (Matthew 25:21).

3. The ultimate benefit and the ultimate glory to God come when a soul is saved because of our obedience (Luke 7:22, I Corinthians 10:33, James 2:18).

4. Every need that comes to our attention is an opportunity to invest one or more of our "talents" to serve God's purpose (Galatians 6:9-10).

When Jesus shared this with His disciples, He was preparing them for a life of ministry without Him. They naively wanted promotion and prosperity in this world (Mark 10:28-30). He wanted something far better and far more eternal for them (and for us).

So here it is in "God Math". Whatever God has given you will be exponentially multiplied when you give it to others, particularly when you let God get the glory (Proverbs 22:9, Luke 6:38, Acts 20:35).

Hang onto it for your own benefit, and it's value will be fleeting and finite (Mark 8:35, Luke 12:16-21). Put it to work for God's purposes, and the value will be eternal (Matthew 6:19-21).

Life is not a talent show, but the Lord does care a great deal about what you have to show for the talents that He's given you. Look for needs that you can meet. Invest in others, and build a Kingdom that you can't see, for a King who *always* sees you.

YOUR PRESCRIPTION

Are there any blessings, gifts, or resources that you've been hoarding for your own benefit? Ask God to show you the things that He wants you to start using for the benefit of others. Direct your resources for His purposes, and He'll do the rest.

SELF EXAMINATION

Is God speaking to you about a problem with your heart?

_____

_____

_____

_____

_____

TREATMENT PLAN

What steps do you need to take to address your heart problem?

_____

_____

_____

_____

_____

In His Hands

"Though I walk in the midst of trouble, thou wilt revive me: thou shalt stretch forth thine hand against the wrath of mine enemies, and thy right hand shall save me." – Psalm 138:7

"And immediately Jesus stretched forth his hand, and caught him, and said unto him, O thou of little faith, wherefore didst thou doubt?"
– Matthew 14:31

"Away then, all fears, the Kingdom is safe in the King's hands." – C.H. Spurgeon

Scripture Reading: Mark 6:7-13, 31-52

When it comes to problems or concerns or dilemmas of any kind, I've never been good at a hands-off approach. I tend to be the white-knuckled type who tries (usually in vain) to bring the situation under control (namely, my own control). And in the end, I only find out how little control I really have.

In Mark 6, Jesus' disciples were white-knuckled. After returning from their first missions trip (Verses 7-13), they had served as waiters to 5000 people, fed by a little boy's lunch and the power of Jesus (Verses 31-44). Jesus then put them in a boat and sent them to cross the Sea of Galilee, while He stayed behind to finish His goodbyes with the well-fed 5000, before going off by Himself to pray (Verses 45-46).

By evening, the disciples are in the middle of the sea, Jesus is watching from the shore, and the winds have kicked up. Here's where the white knuckles come in. In spite of the power that had been given to them, and the power they had seen on display, the disciples were now over-powered by fear. And worse still, they were fighting the wind and the waves in their own power - and they were losing (Verses 47-48).

The fact that Jesus came walking on the water in the "fourth watch" tells us that these guys had been "toiling" in their own strength for most of the night. They were so shaken up by the storm that they couldn't even recognize their own Salvation walking on the water, and they first thought Jesus was a ghost (which, of course, only shook them up even more).

But notice the contrast in Jesus' reaction. He's not rattled. He's not even running. He walks to them on the water (the waves are no threat to Him), tells them to "be of good cheer" (the exact opposite of what they were at that moment), and steps into the boat. And once He enters the boat, His mere presence is enough to bring the storm to a screeching halt.

I really can't fault the disciples for their next response, because I catch myself doing the same thing. Their next response is to be *amazed*, as if they had never seen such great power exercised on their behalf before, when in truth, they had seen the power of God in action earlier that day, and the day before that, and the day before that.

I suppose white knuckles are a part of being human, but can I tell you, they're a waste of energy in the presence of Almighty God. When He tells us to cast our cares on Him, He really means it, and He is more than able to handle it without our help, thank you very much.

Think back (and I doubt you'll have to think back far). Who has He provided for in your presence? Who has He healed?

Who has He changed? Who has He blessed and rescued and made Himself real to? I'm sure if we were all together in a room, we could share some amazing stories with each other about all we have seen Him do.

And yet, at every bump in the road, we stumble and forget His greatness, and we "toil" in vain to fix our own road, rather than letting Him take over.

And so, in conclusion, I'll tell you what I have to tell myself nearly every day for one reason or another. Put the problem in His Hands. Put the solution in His Hands. Put your fears, your assumptions, your desires, and everything that you *think* should happen in His Hands.

Stop trying to figure it all out. *No really, just stop.* It's so simple. He is so Sovereign – and anything and everything that we manage to entrust to Him is absolutely, undoubtedly, and ever-amazingly safe – in His all-sufficient Hands.

YOUR PRESCRIPTION

Remember what God has done. Better yet, tell someone else what God has done for you. When you testify about His good-ness, you encourage someone else and encourage yourself at the same time. Don't let today's struggles rob you of tomor-row's blessings.

SELF EXAMINATION
Is God speaking to you about a problem with your heart?

_____

_____

_____

_____

_____

TREATMENT PLAN
What steps do you need to take to address your heart problem?

_____

_____

_____

_____

_____

Doormats & Dirty Feet

"But love ye your enemies, and do good, and lend, hoping for nothing again; and your reward shall be great, and ye shall be the children of the Highest: for he is kind unto the unthankful and to the evil. Be ye therefore merciful, as your Father also is merciful." - Luke 6:35-36

"Who, being in the form of God, thought it not robbery to be equal with God: But made himself of no reputation, and took upon him the form of a servant, and was made in the likeness of men: And being found in fashion as a man, he humbled himself, and became obedient unto death, even the death of the cross." - Philippians 2:6-8

Scripture Reading: John 13:1-17

I've never thought of myself as a proud person. I'm always overworked, overcommitted, and overwhelmed, so if anything, I thought I was a doormat. And yet, as I get older, I'm starting to realize just how many of my thoughts and responses are fueled by some form of pride, and frankly, I'm not proud of it.

Too many times, I catch myself being indignant (on the inside) that anyone would have the nerve to expect *this* from me, or to say *that* to me, or to assume *this* about me, or to dump *that* in my lap. **Sound familiar?** I hate to break it to you, my friend (and I assure you that we're in this together), but those are the subtle echoes of pride in our everyday lives, and they really *don't* echo the life of Jesus (Proverbs 13:10, 27:15).

In John 13, on the eve of His crucifixion, Jesus shattered any ideas that you and I might have about our own dignity, pride, and position. He did it with a towel, a bowl of water, and a bunch of dirty feet.

Verse 1 makes it clear that Jesus' actions were fueled by love, even though He was fully aware that His disciples would soon scatter in "every man for himself" fashion. Verse 3 makes it clear that He was confident in His position, knowing that His Father had given all things into His hands. And yet, Jesus was about to demonstrate a humility that is almost beyond comprehension (Philippians 2:6-8).

In human terms, He is their leader. In heavenly terms, He is the Son of God. And yet, He takes the role of a servant - not the head servant, but the last and lowliest servant in the pecking order - and with towel in hand, He kneels before each of them and washes their feet.

There was no misunderstanding why He did it, either. In Verses 12-16, He plainly states that it was an "example" for their sakes. It was part and parcel of what they would have to do to be like Him, to please Him, and even to "be happy".

Really??? Happiness is being a doormat? That's a hard pill to swallow, but let me put it to you this way. As I look at myself, I know that I have no happiness - only gloom, despair, and agony - when I am focused on all that I think I deserve. When I'm trying to prove to others that I deserve better, somehow, I only end up feeling worse. But when I find my security in God's sovereignty, His peace overshadows my pride. And when I'm trying to be a little *more* like Jesus and a little *less* like the world around me, He gives me a wonderfully odd and unnatural contentment - in any circumstance (Philippians 2:3, 4:6-12, Hebrews 13:5).

When I trade my pride for His peace, my pride not only hurts a little less, it actually comes out a little less (I Timothy 1:7, 6:6, I Peter 5:6).

But there's more to this. As I become more Christ-like in my responses, the weird, counter-cultural unnaturalness of it all draws other people to Him (John 3:14-15). That's a sobering thought. Probably the only thing worse than letting your pride keep you from salvation would be if your pride kept other people from finding salvation. God forbid that my self-serving attitude should ever drive anyone away from His grace. You may not like the idea of being a doormat, but at the very least, make sure you are a welcome mat that brings people to the Door (John 10:9), and the Way, the Truth, and the Life (John 14:6).

So I guess it all comes down to towels. When it comes to your pride, throw in the towel (I John 2:16). When it comes to others, pick up a towel and start serving (Galatians 6:2). And when you start to think of yourself as a doormat, remember the dirty feet that you came with, and the Savior who washes them clean.

YOUR PRESCRIPTION

Is there a situation right now where your pride is getting in the way? Ask God to help you to respond in a humble way. God will not promote you until you stop promoting yourself. And trust me, His plans and His promotions are better.

SELF EXAMINATION
Is God speaking to you about a problem with your heart?

_____

_____

_____

_____

_____

TREATMENT PLAN
What steps do you need to take to address your heart problem?

_____

_____

_____

_____

_____

Ready to Run

"Blessed is the man that walketh not in the counsel of the ungodly, nor standeth in the way of sinners, nor sitteth in the seat of the scornful. But his delight is in the law of the Lord; and in his law doth he meditate day and night."
- Psalm 1:1-2

"Let your light so shine before men, that they may see your good works, and glorify your Father which is in heaven." - Matthew 5:16

"Submit yourselves therefore to God. Resist the devil, and he will flee from you." - James 4:7

Scripture Reading: Genesis 39

I have a special gift for making excuses, and to my shame, I'm sometimes better at making excuses, rather than simply doing what I know needs to be done.

Maybe that's why I'm so impressed with Joseph. In spite of really rotten brothers, unfair enslavement and imprisonment, along with years of immersion in an ungodly culture, Joseph lived a life of "no excuses". Whenever the Lord opened a door for Joseph, he was ready to do right, and when Satan tried to trap him with an opportunity for evil, Joseph was ready to run.

By God's grace, Joseph always rose to the top of the heap. In one of the Bible's most notorious dysfunctional families, Joseph was the stand-out and his father Jacob's favorite (Genesis 37:3-4). His dreams about his divine destiny angered his brothers and even insulted his father (Verses 5-10), but Jacob couldn't deny that God had something planned for this boy (Verse 11).

When his enraged brothers finally sold him to Midianite traders (Genesis 37:26, 36), God's favor turned Joseph's slavery into a successful career, as he became the trusted caretaker of one of Egypt's most prestigious households (Genesis 39:2-5). But temptation tends to lurk in the shadows of prosperity, and one of the greatest tests of Joseph's character was yet to come in the advances of Potiphar's wife (Genesis 39:7-9).

Like most temptations, Potiphar's wife was distracting, convenient, and persistent. She followed him everywhere, waiting for a weak moment (Genesis 39:10). If Joseph had given in, he could have made endless excuses for his actions (our society certainly would have given him a pass - Proverbs 30:11-14). But rather than sugarcoat the situation, Joseph used words like "sin" and "wickedness" in Genesis 39:9 (words that don't get enough use these days) and avoided her like the plague. And when she finally cornered him, he literally ran from her grip (Genesis 39:10-12).

Sometimes I think that we don't run often enough. We qualify, compromise, and coexist with sin. We get all too comfortable in this world, even though we know it's not our home (John 15:18-19, Hebrews 11:13, James 4:4).

And as for our temptations, while they may not be the stuff that movies are made of, they are no less persistent than Potiphar's wife, and certainly no less convenient. They're as close as the living room and the dinner table, the company you keep (Psalm 1), and the thoughts you entertain (Proverbs 4:23, Romans 12:2).

For instance, who brings out the worst in you? It's no coincidence that you'll come face-to-face with that person in your most frustrated, exhausted moment (Proverbs 25:28, Ephesians 4:29, 32). And if you watch TV, keep the remote well within reach, as it will take 90 seconds or less for something morally offensive to flash across the screen and pollute your mind (Romans 8:6-7, Philippians 4:8).

And what about the temptations that seem to be a part of our very makeup - the critical thoughts, the angry words, the pride, the lies, envy, and feelings of despair. They *seem* petty and harmless on the inside, but once they work their way to the surface, their potential for disaster is unlimited.

When sin tries to grab a hold of you, *be ready to run* (I Corinthians 6:18, II Timothy 2:22, I Peter 5:8, James 4:7). Run to God's Word for the truth you need to face the persistent temptations of an immoral world (Psalm 119:11). And run to the "psalms, hymns, and spiritual songs" (Colossians 3:16) for strength and comfort in the face of the distractions within.

There is a time for everything under heaven (Ecclesiastes 3:1-8). Know when it's time to run. Run away from the temptations of this world, run the race that is set before you (Philippians 3:13-14, Hebrews 12:1-2), and run to the Throne for help in time of need (Hebrews 4:16).

And when your race is finally done, run all the way Home (Psalm 37:24).

YOUR PRESCRIPTION

Are you struggling with a temptation right now? Whether you realize it or not, the real battleground is your mind. Make a conscious, deliberate effort to fill your thoughts with scripture, prayer, and songs about your Savior. Nothing drives your Enemy away faster than a mind set on the things of God.

SELF EXAMINATION

Is God speaking to you about a problem with your heart?

_____

_____

_____

_____

_____

TREATMENT PLAN

What steps do you need to take to address your heart problem?

_____

_____

_____

_____

_____

Lessons from the Waiting Room

*"Wait on the Lord: be of good courage, and he
shall strengthen thine heart: wait, I say, on the
Lord." - Psalm 27:14*

*"Cast thy burden upon the Lord, and he shall
sustain thee: he shall never suffer the righteous
to be moved." - Psalm 55:22*

*"But they that wait upon the Lord shall renew
their strength; they shall mount up with wings
as eagles; they shall run, and not be weary; and
they shall walk, and not faint." - Isaiah 40:31*

Scripture Reading: Psalm 37

I'm hanging out in God's waiting room with some dear
friends of mine. I'm here because I know firsthand how
hard it is to wait. I'm also here because I owe them the favor,
as they've waited with me on more than one occasion. Prayers
have gone up. Tears have been shed. Hearts are heavy, and from
a human standpoint, the answers seem to be taking forever.

God is faithful, but His timetable often (almost always)
differs from ours. If you're waiting on answers today, here are

a few lessons from God's waiting room to help you pass the time and trust His timing:

1. **Everything has an order** (Psalm 30:5, 138:7-8, Ecclesiastes 3:1, 11). You walk into a waiting room, sign the clipboard at the reception desk, and start waiting. And while you may be frustrated to see so many other names ahead of yours, take comfort in the fact that no name will be ignored and every need will be addressed in the proper order. You may not like the order, but unlike your earthly appointments, the order here is perfect.

2. **Keep an open mind** (Psalm 37:3-7, James 1:3-5). Has it ever occurred to you that you might not be praying for the right thing? Our prayers are usually driven by our personal agendas and our very limited (and often deluded) understanding of what's best. Spend the time waiting in prayer (rather than worrying) and God will gradually bring your desires into alignment with His will. The more time you spend in His presence, the more your requests will resemble His intentions - and that's a very good thing.

3. **Make yourself comfortable** (Romans 12:10-12). Don't be ashamed or annoyed or insulted that God asks you to wait. Realize that His delays are not denials. Rather, they are invitations to get to know Him better. Get comfortable in God's waiting room. There is music playing overhead (Zephaniah 3:17), a water cooler (Psalm 23:2), great reading material (Psalm 119:11), and a comfortable seat in the refuge of His wings (Psalm 17:8).

4. **Your name will be called when you least expect it** (Psalm 3:4, 34:4-5, 86:13, 121). Instead of just waiting for the specific answer you've requested, ask God to make you sensitive to His every leading in your situation. The picture is always bigger from His perspective, and He may want to teach you things that you never expected to learn. More than that, while you're in the midst of your need, He may use you to minister to the needs of others. That's a blessing that gives purpose to your pain.

5. **You will always get what you need** (Psalm 16:5, Isaiah 61:7, Matthew 6:8, 31-34). God is a good Father who loves His children. Never doubt that. He will not set you up for failure, and He never allows a need in your life that He doesn't fully intend to meet. To prove it, He often meets one need with many blessings, and leaves us not only satisfied, but saturated, with His goodness.

6. **You'll never have to wait alone** (Psalm 34:18, Isaiah 41:13). God is for you. God is with you. God loves you beyond your comprehension. He is in the waiting room with you, holding your hand, whispering words of comfort, and gently pleading with you to wait on His perfect timing for His end.

If you're in God's waiting room today, my heart goes out to you, but please know that you're in good company. Make no mistake about it, His waiting room and His Throne Room are one in the same (Hebrews 4:16), and whatever your need, if you have lifted it up in prayer, then it is in the hands of the Sovereign King. Trust His power, trust His plan, trust His timing. And most of all - trust His heart.

YOUR PRESCRIPTION

Instead of asking God to end your wait, ask Him what He wants to accomplish in you and through you while you wait. Know that once HIS desires for you have been accomplished, the wait will be over.

SELF EXAMINATION
Is God speaking to you about a problem with your heart?

_____

_____

_____

_____

_____

TREATMENT PLAN
What steps do you need to take to address your heart problem?

_____

_____

_____

_____

_____

Perception & Reality

"And the serpent said unto the woman, Ye shall not surely die: For God doth know that in the day ye eat thereof, then your eyes shall be opened, and ye shall be as gods, knowing good and evil." - Genesis 3:4-5

"Hold up my goings in thy paths, that my footsteps slip not...Keep me as the apple of the eye, hide me under the shadow of thy wings."
                                    - Psalm 17:5, 8

"But I fear, lest by any means, as the serpent beguiled Eve through his subtilty, so your minds should be corrupted from the simplicity that is in Christ." - II Corinthians 11:3

Scripture Reading: Genesis 3:1-20

It's been said that perception is reality. That's an interesting thought, but I don't buy it. While it's tempting to think that you or I can define our own truth, weave our own wisdom, and render our own reality, that very premise was disastrously bought by Eve back in the garden of Eden. It didn't end well then, and I don't believe it bodes any better for us today.

When the serpent approached Eve in Genesis 3, he immediately went to work on her perception of God, and with just a few clever drops of deception, that seed of doubt quickly grew into a root of bitterness (Hebrews 12:15).

The premise was simple - God can't be trusted (Genesis 3:4-5). He *doesn't* give you His best, and He *doesn't* know what's best for you.

Satan played on some character traits in Eve that still lurk in our DNA today. He played on her need for control, her need to feel that she could understand everything on her own terms, and her desire to be so self-sufficient that she didn't need God (much less a man) to provide for her. And by assigning reality to Eve's flawed perception, Satan pulled off an incredible con in the Garden of Eden. He got Eve to doubt the goodness of God, the plan of God, and her place in it.

Satan's tactics haven't really changed all that much, and he still tries to pull that same con job on women like you and me. He tries to make us believe that our destiny is in our own feeble hands, or that our future is already a lost cause or a foregone conclusion because of what someone else has done to us, or because of the cards that "fate" (the buzz-word used by the world to deny God's sovereignty) has dealt us.

Lies, lies, and more lies (John 8:44, I Corinthians 1:21, 3:19).

Is Satan messing with your perception of God today? If so, let me lay out the truth. God is *not* holding out on you (Psalm 34:8, 84:11, Romans 8:32). You are not stuck or trapped or doomed to failure. If you have accepted Christ as your Savior, you are a Child of the King, and the apple of His eye (Psalm 17:8, 77:8-10, I John 3:1). If Eve had realized she was the apple of God's eye, if she had only remembered how precious and loved and cherished she was, she wouldn't have seen anything worth having in the fruit that Satan offered.

And let me remind you of the reality of your enemy (I Peter 5:8). Don't believe the hype. While you must always be aware of his persistence, don't allow him to distort your perception of him. In reality, he is just another one of God's created beings (Romans 1:25, I John 3:20, 4:4). He is not anywhere *close* to being equal with God, and he can be overcome.

As women, we have a need to process our thoughts and emotions, and it's a process that Satan always tries to contaminate. Sometimes we process internally, and Satan tries to poison our thoughts with doubts, paranoia, criticism, and insecurity. Sometimes we process externally by talking with others. Satan will try to contaminate this process, too, turning our conversation into gossip, backbiting, and negative reinforcement, (the equally effective and direct opposite of positive reinforcement).

My advice to you - *always process your emotions through prayer*. When circumstances are beyond your understanding and you're tempted to doubt God's goodness, get a grip on reality, by getting a hold on His promises (Romans 12:2).

Don't let your emotions, your ambitions, your pride, or your insecurities be the perception that defines your reality. God is Who He says He is. He does what He promises to do (Hebrews 11:6). And you can trust Him *with* everything and *in* everything that concerns you (Psalm 27:1, 138:8, Proverbs 3:5-6).

YOUR PRESCRIPTION

Don't be afraid to take your doubts and your questions to God. He wants to speak to your fears and show you the reality of Who He is. Process your emotions, your concerns, and your questions through prayer, and God will honor your desire to seek Him in your situation.

SELF EXAMINATION
Is God speaking to you about a problem with your heart?

_____

_____

_____

_____

_____

TREATMENT PLAN
What steps do you need to take to address your heart problem?

_____

_____

_____

_____

_____

Scarred for Life

"But he was wounded for our transgressions, he was bruised for our iniquities: the chastisement of our peace was upon him; and with his stripes we are healed." - Isaiah 53:5

"Then saith he to Thomas, Reach hither thy finger, and behold my hands; and reach hither thy hand, and thrust it into my side: and be not faithless, but believing. And Thomas answered and said unto him, My Lord and my God."
- John 20:27-28

"Therefore I take pleasure in infirmities, in reproaches, in necessities, in persecutions, in distresses for Christ's sake: for when I am weak, then am I strong." - II Corinthians 12:10

Scripture Reading: John 20:19-31

It's easy to knock Thomas.

He was the guy who could never take anything at face value, the guy who always raised his hand to ask one more question when everyone else was ready to just move on. His persistence served us well in John 14, as Jesus erased all doubt about the way to heaven by declaring Himself as the Way, the Truth, and the Life, and the only Way to the Father (John 14:6).

And in John 20, Thomas's insistence that he had to touch the scars of Jesus with his own hands gives us some insight into the eternal impact of scars.

As a kid growing up in church, there were some things that just didn't make sense to me. I remember questioning in my mind (though I never had the guts to ask the question aloud) why Jesus had scars on His hands and side (John 20:20). After all, He was God. He had healed others, and more than once, the gospel writers used the phrase "made whole" (Matthew 9:22, Mark 6:56, 10:52, John 5:15), implying that there was no residue of illness or infirmity left behind when He healed someone. So why was Christ Himself scarred for all of eternity?

A few years and a few scars of my own have helped me to understand that God *chose* to keep those scars for our sakes. If you feel as though you have somehow been scarred for life, let me tell you why your Savior chose to keep His scars and what He wants to do with yours.

1. **Proof of Life.** For Thomas, even multiple eyewitness accounts weren't good enough. Although the other disciples had seen and spoken to Christ a week earlier, Thomas needed personal sensory proof that Jesus was alive. Touching the scars proved that Jesus's human body had been resurrected. He was not a ghost or a dream. He was the same God-in-the-flesh that had hung on the cross, and He was alive again. One day, we will see those scars, and we too will know that our Redeemer lives (Job 19:25, Psalm 22:16, Zechariah 13:6, Revelation 5:12).

2. **Proof of Love.** If you are scarred, you are in good company. The only person God ever expected to suffer alone was Jesus Christ (Isaiah 54:7-8, Matthew 27:46).

For every trial and tribulation that you and I face, God is there - passing through the fire with us (Isaiah 43:2), collecting our tears (Psalm 56:8), and providing new mercies every morning (Lamentations 3:21-23). We may not understand why He allows certain hurts and heartaches, but He still carries the scars that He sustained on our behalf, and He never fails to carry us. No matter how bad life in this fallen world may seem, I guarantee you that it would be far worse without the protection and provision of those nail-scarred hands. And unlike those scars, our trials are only temporary (Isaiah 49:16, John 16:33, II Corinthians 4:17).

3. **Proof of Purchase.** Jesus purchased our redemption with those scars, but His scars also add value to ours. Just as His scars have eternal impact on our lives, our ugliest and deepest scars can have eternal impact in the lives of others. Pain has purpose in His nail-scarred hands, and you can be the light that leads a soul with similar sufferings to new life in Christ (II Corinthians 1:4, 4:7, 5:17, 6:20, I Timothy 1:15, I Peter 2:9).

As Christians, we sometimes put a lot of effort into hiding our scars. We're so afraid to let others see them, that we fail to see how God wants to use those scars - not for our own glory, but for *His*.

I'm not proud of my scars, but I praise God for His. And I pray that I can be humble enough to show someone else my scars to prove that He lives in me, He loves me, and I belong to Him.

YOUR PRESCRIPTION

Praise God for His scars and ask Him to give you an opportunity to use your trials and tribulations - past and present - for His glory.

SELF EXAMINATION
Is God speaking to you about a problem with your heart?

_____

_____

_____

_____

_____

TREATMENT PLAN
What steps do you need to take to address your heart problem?

_____

_____

_____

_____

_____

Walk a Mile

"But a certain Samaritan, as he journeyed, came where he was: and when he saw him, he had compassion on him, And went to him, and bound up his wounds, pouring in oil and wine, and set him on his own beast, and brought him to an inn, and took care of him." - Luke 10:33-34

"Rejoice with them that do rejoice, and weep with them that weep." - Romans 12:15

"The Spirit of the Lord God is upon me; because the Lord hath anointed me to preach good tidings unto the meek; he hath sent me to bind up the brokenhearted, to proclaim liberty to the captives, and the opening of the prison to them that are bound; To proclaim the acceptable year of the Lord, and the day of vengeance of our God; to comfort all that mourn; To appoint unto them that mourn in Zion, to give unto them beauty for ashes, the oil of joy for mourning, the garment of praise for the spirit of heaviness; that they might be called trees of righteousness, the planting of the Lord, that he might be glorified." - Isaiah 61:1-3

Scripture Reading: Luke 10:25-37

I t never hurts to walk a mile in someone else's shoes. In fact, it can do you a world of good.

In the parable of the Good Samaritan in Luke 10, Jesus illustrates the concept of loving your neighbor as yourself, and it strikes me that it involves more than just talk. It involves deliberate action, deliberate involvement, and deliberate steps in their direction.

You know the story. A man is left on the side of the road for dead. Robbed and beaten, this poor soul is in desperate need of help. Ironically, two religious icons of the day - a priest and a Levite - each stumble across the victim in turn. Both move to the other side of the road, avoiding any involvement with the man's plight and continuing on their own self-centered way.

The hero of our story is someone that Jesus' audience would have considered a "dog".

Samaritans were hated by Jews, but this man put his Jewish counterparts to shame. The Samaritan traveler not only has compassion - he takes action. With no regard for his own schedule or his own obligations, this man completely puts himself in the shoes of the wounded man. He stops in his tracks and redirects - not just his thoughts and prayers - but his time, money, and his own mode of transportation ("set him on his own beast") in order to meet the man's needs. And the commitment is long-term, as he promises to return again to pay any additional expenses.

Let's think for a minute about what the Samaritan *didn't* do. He *didn't* hesitate. He *didn't* count the cost (Proverbs 3:27). He *didn't* stop to evaluate whether or not this man deserved his help (Matthew 7:1-3). He *didn't* wait for someone else to take the lead or to put a stamp of approval on his actions.

He saw. He felt. And he moved.

When we pray for God to meet the needs of others, do we consider that He may want to meet those needs through us?

When Jesus felt compassion (Matthew 9:36, 14:14, Mark 1:41), it always moved Him to take action. When the Lord moves *your* heart with compassion, know that He is trying to get you to move, too (Psalm 143:10, Matthew 25:34-40, Galatians 6:10, Ephesians 2:10, James 1:27).

One last thought. We can judge the priest and the Levite all day long, but how often do you and I keep a safe distance from hurting people?

I know I have failed on more than one occasion to get my hands dirty, sacrifice my time, and walk a mile in someone else's painful shoes. There have been times that I didn't know what to say to someone, so I avoided having to face them at all. Other times, I was too selfish to give up my own time, my own comfort, or I was too lazy to make a commitment. Worse still, there were times when I judged someone else to be less than deserving of my help for reasons that would probably never hold up with God. After all, He has never based His dealings with me on what *I* deserve (Romans 5:8, Philippians 2:12-13, Titus 3:5), and I'd be in sorry shape if He did.

Don't just pray for God to move. *Pray for Him to move you.* When you pray for the hurting, ask God to use you to help them. Don't expect that the Good Samaritan will be one or two people behind you on the road. Make a conscious effort to be ready, willing, and available for God to work through you (Romans 12:15, Galatians 6:2, I John 5:1-2).

Hurting people are left lying on the roadside of life every day. Instead of weaving our way around them, let's stop, pick them up, and walk a mile in their shoes.

You just might realize how blessed you are, once you take the time to stop and be a blessing to someone else (Psalm 89:1, Jeremiah 9:24).

YOUR PRESCRIPTION

Take the time to care for the hurting people in your path. Pray for them, but be the sympathetic ear, the helping hands, and the generous heart that is the answer to their prayers. God will bless you for it.

SELF EXAMINATION
Is God speaking to you about a problem with your heart?

_____

_____

_____

_____

_____

TREATMENT PLAN
What steps do you need to take to address your heart problem?

_____

_____

_____

_____

The Greenest Grass

"And Lot lifted up his eyes, and beheld all the plain of Jordan, that it was well watered every where, before the Lord destroyed Sodom and Gomorrah, even as the garden of the Lord, like the land of Egypt, as thou comest unto Zoar. Then Lot chose him all the plain of Jordan; and Lot journeyed east: and they separated themselves the one from the other." - Genesis 3:10-11

"Thou wilt shew me the path of life: in thy presence is fulness of joy; at thy right hand there are pleasures for evermore." - Psalm 16:11

"The Lord is my shepherd; I shall not want. He maketh me to lie down in green pastures…"
- Psalm 23:1-2a

Scripture Reading: Genesis 19:1-28

I am often overwhelmed by the goodness of God. When I think back on some of the foolish roads that I've gone down - when I remember the times that He pursued me, when I was pursuing everything *but* Him - I am just amazed at the patience, the mercy, and the extreme kindness of our God.

There was a time when I believed the lie that the grass is greener outside of God's will. That's why I so often stress the need to understand that God's timetable is different from ours. As a young woman, I was forever hung up on my own timetable. I wanted to be married by 25, a mom by 27, and so on, and when God didn't deliver those things according to my expectations, I soon set out in search of greener pastures.

I wonder if Lot's wife thought the same way. We don't know much about her, but one thing becomes abundantly clear in Genesis 19 - somewhere along the way, she fell in love with life outside of God's will.

Her husband had started out on the right road. As Abraham's nephew, Lot had joined his uncle on the journey out of Haran (Genesis 13:1). Maybe even then, he was in search of greener pastures than the life he was born into, but at least he seemed to be following Abraham, who was certainly following God.

But that actually brings up a very important point. Faith has to be personal, and your faith must be your own - not the extension of someone else's. Ride the train of someone else's faith, and your faith will easily go off the rails, especially when temptation comes on board. Abraham's faith only carries Lot for so long, and when strife breaks out between the two, it doesn't take long for Lot to start looking for the next big thing.

The truth is, we don't hear about Lot's wife in any of this. She's not mentioned when her husband decides to move east (Genesis 13:9-12), or when he takes the life-changing step of pitching his tent "toward Sodom". She's such a silent partner in the destruction of her family that we don't even know her name (Proverbs 14:1).

But her restless and worldly heart is revealed in two brief, but powerful statements (Proverbs 14:12, John 15:19, I John 2:15).

The first is in Genesis 19:26, "But his wife looked back from behind him..." Lot had lingered in leaving Sodom and Gomorrah behind, according to verse 16, so much so that the angels took he and his wife and daughters by their hands, literally dragging them away from destruction. But Lot's wife lingered all the more, bringing up the rear, and eventually directly disobeying the command to not look back (Verse 17). That look results in her immediate destruction, and sets the ultimate destruction of her husband and daughters (later in Chapter 19) in motion.

The second statement about Lot's wife is made by Jesus, Himself. In Luke 17:32, He uses Lot's wife as a cautionary tale for His disciples, and with the three little words, "Remember Lot's wife", He speaks to all of us who have to choose between a life in God's will and a life of our own making (Luke 17:33).

Make no mistake about it - the grass is greenest in the will of God (Psalm 16:11, 19:8-10, 23:2, Isaiah 54:1, 4). I cannot plead with you enough - don't buy the lie that this world has something better to offer. Don't think for a minute that you are deprived, or that you are missing out in some way.

God's plan is best. God's timing is perfect. And if you stay close to Him, the things He has for you are more than you could ask for or imagine. Walk in His way. Wait on His will, and never, ever look back.

YOUR PRESCRIPTION

Know that God has not left your situation, and know that His plan for you is in motion - even when you can't see it. Ask Him to help you to wait on Him, rather than running to the quick fix that the world has to offer. God is a good Father, a good Provider, and He is faithful.

SELF EXAMINATION
Is God speaking to you about a problem with your heart?

_____

_____

_____

_____

_____

TREATMENT PLAN
What steps do you need to take to address your heart problem?

_____

_____

_____

_____

_____

So I Prayed

"Then the king said unto me, For what dost thou make request? So I prayed to the God of heaven." - Nehemiah 2:4

"Yet the Lord will command his lovingkindness in the day time, and in the night his song shall be with me, and my prayer unto the God of my life." - Psalm 42:8

"Be careful for nothing; but in every thing by prayer and supplication with thanksgiving let your requests be made known unto God. And the peace of God, which passeth all understanding, shall keep your hearts and minds through Christ Jesus." - Philippians 4:6-7

Scripture Reading: Nehemiah 2:1-8

I had one of those mornings where everything seemed out of whack and nothing went the way it was supposed to. When our external circumstances are out of line, they quickly reveal any internal lack of alignment, and I have to admit, as my morning spun out of control, so did my attitude. I soon came to the realization that my head and my heart needed to get back in alignment with God.

Nehemiah, on the other hand, was completely *in* alignment with God - inside and out. He loved God, and although he was the faithful cupbearer to the Persian king, his heart was with the people of God back in Jerusalem. He had heard that Jerusalem was in ruins (Nehemiah 1:3-4). The walls were destroyed, and the remnant that was left behind after the Babylonian invasion, some 70 years before, was defenseless and devastated.

But for Nehemiah, prayer was a reflex. His immediate response was to fast and pray - not just for a few minutes, or even a few hours, but for a matter of months. There is a span of about four months between the month of Chisleu, mentioned in Nehemiah 1:1, and the month of Nisan, noted in Nehemiah 2:1. During that span, Nehemiah prayed without ceasing. He prayed for forgiveness for himself and his people. He prayed the promises of God, and he prayed for favor in the sight of the king (Nehemiah 1:5-6).

Nehemiah's prayer instincts are well exercised by the time he has his long-awaited conversation with the king in Chapter 2. And so, with no time to even think about it, his prayer reflex kicks in once again.

When the king inquires about Nehemiah's obvious distress (Verses 2-3), Nehemiah has the knee-jerk response that often eludes even the most well-meaning Christians (Verse 4), "So I prayed to the God of heaven." And as He still promises us today, God honors Nehemiah's prayer, granting him the king's favor and everything else that the journey to Jerusalem required (Verse 8).

While Nehemiah was praying about really big stuff like a city in ruins and people in peril, his example applies to the big, obvious problems in our lives, as well as the hidden heart problems we struggle with on a daily basis.

My hope is this. For every challenge, big or small, I want my spontaneous, reflexive reaction to be, "So I prayed to the

God of heaven." I was worried about something, so I prayed to the God of heaven (Philippians 4:6-7, I Peter 5:6-7). Somebody upset me, so I prayed to the God of heaven (Psalm 6:2). I wasn't sure what to do, so I prayed to the God of heaven (Psalm 32:8, Proverbs 3:5-6, James 1:5). My thoughts started to go in the wrong direction, so I prayed to the God of heaven (Psalm 51:6, Jeremiah 17:9).

It's simple. When I go it alone, I end up trying to force everything to line up with my will. When I go to God in prayer, I align myself with His will and leave the outcomes to Him. I have learned that only one thing moves my hard heart, and my even harder head, back into line. That one thing is prayer.

As you move through your day, strengthen your prayer reflex every chance you get. Fight the inner reflexes of complaining, criticizing, worrying, and wanting with spontaneous prayer (Matthew 26:41, Philippians 4:8, Colossians 3:2, 4:2). Pray for forgiveness, pray the promises of God, and pray for His will, His guidance, and His favor in everything that concerns you (Psalm 5:12, 106:4).

I had a rough morning today, so I prayed to the God of heaven. I couldn't stop complaining about my rough morning, so I prayed to the God of heaven. And though I didn't deserve His help, God was faithful, and He kept His promise to give me peace in the midst of it all (Isaiah 26:3). And so, I prayed and *praised* the God of heaven (Hebrews 13:15).

YOUR PRESCRIPTION

Pray that prayer will become your strongest reflex. Ask God to bring you to the place where you bring everything to His throne - all day, every day.

SELF EXAMINATION
Is God speaking to you about a problem with your heart?

_____

_____

_____

_____

_____

TREATMENT PLAN
What steps do you need to take to address your heart problem?

_____

_____

_____

_____

_____

King of Hearts

"I will go before thee, and make the crooked places straight: I will break in pieces the gates of brass, and cut in sunder the bars of iron: And I will give thee the treasures of darkness, and hidden riches of secret places, that thou mayest know that I, the Lord, which call thee by thy name, am the God of Israel." - Isaiah 45:2-3

"The king's heart is in the hand of the Lord, as the rivers of water: he turneth it whithersoever he will." - Proverbs 21:1

"And he changeth the times and the seasons: he removeth kings, and setteth up kings: he giveth wisdom unto the wise, and knowledge to them that know understanding…" - Daniel 2:21

Scripture Reading: II Chronicles 36

Just a few short days ago, I felt very cornered. My husband and I had to make some critical decisions.

We had prayed and others were praying with us, the end result was not good. But then, that wasn't the end. Just as we were ready to take a huge loss, a phone call came. And then everything changed.

There was no doubt in my mind that God had intervened. Someone's heart had been turned 180 degrees (in our favor), and I knew that it wasn't our doing - it was the Lord's.

In II Chronicles 36, we get a summary of the events sandwiched between the reigns of two very different kings. The Chapter starts after the death of Josiah, the boy-king (his reign started at the age of 8). Josiah was a breath of fresh air in the history of Judah. Chapters 34-35 recount his faithfulness to the ways of God. He abolished idol worship and repaired the temple. And when he found the long-lost Books of the Law (scriptures), Josiah read them to the people and led them in keeping their covenant with God.

But after Josiah's death, everything goes downhill. Rebellion returns, and with God's commandments ignored, the worst of prophecies come true at the hands of Nebuchadnezzar and the Babylonians (Jeremiah 25). Seventy years of captivity ensue, while Jerusalem lies in waste.

But I mentioned two kings that bookend this period. The second is not a Jewish king. He is a Persian king. Cyrus is at the top of his game. It is his first year as king (around 539 B.C.), and with the Babylonian Empire long gone, he now rules the largest empire that the world has known to date.

But Someone is more Sovereign than Cyrus. Another prophecy comes true (II Chronicles 36:22-23, Ezra 1:1-3, Isaiah 44:28), and Cyrus takes a complete departure from the foreign kings that Judah has known for the last seventy years. He sets the Jews free. They are free to return to Jerusalem, free to rebuild the city, and free to rebuild the house of the Lord. The rebuilding is even bank-rolled by Cyrus's treasury (Ezra 7:6).

This incredible turn of events is not man's doing. Cyrus himself notes in Ezra 1:2 that the Lord gave him both his kingdom *and* this historic assignment, and the Lord refers to Cyrus as His "anointed" in Isaiah 45:1.

The point? God is the King of Kings, the King of Hearts, and the Sovereign Lord of everything (Isaiah 54:15-17, Revelation 17:14, 19:16).

Once you wrap your head around it, there's immeasurable comfort in God's sovereignty. Sovereignty helps me sleep at night, because everything that seems impossible isn't (Psalm 121, Proverbs 3:24, Luke 1:37). Everything that seems out of control isn't (Proverbs 16:4, Colossians 1:17, Hebrews 4:13). Everything that seems beyond changing and beyond repair isn't (Isaiah 43:19, Jeremiah 32:27). It's all just another chapter in HIS story.

God raised up Nebuchadnezzar - and took him down (Daniel 4) - and God raised up Cyrus. Every event of the 70-year captivity was orchestrated by God for a purpose. Such are the days of our lives. God is always at work, always on the throne, and always right. Nothing happens outside of His permissive will, and everything serves a purpose in His hands (Romans 8:28).

If you're at the mercy of someone's hardened heart today, I'm here to tell you, that heart is not beyond the mercy of God. Know that it's not outside of His Sovereignty, and not beyond His awesome, heart-turning power. He holds the hearts of kings in His hand, and He holds your future in His hands as well. Stop fighting His plan and His timing. You may not get exactly what you want, but you will get God's perfect will, and that is far better. Take that hard heart (and yours) to the Lord in prayer, and let the King of Hearts have His way.

YOUR PRESCRIPTION

Thank God for the good and the bad in your life. Acknowledge His sovereign power in your life, and ask Him to guide you on the path that He has for you - wherever it takes you.

SELF EXAMINATION
Is God speaking to you about a problem with your heart?

_____

_____

_____

_____

_____

TREATMENT PLAN
What steps do you need to take to address your heart problem?

_____

_____

_____

_____

_____

Digging Deep

"And Ruth said, Intreat me not to leave thee, or to return from following after thee: for whither thou goest, I will go; and where thou lodgest, I will lodge: thy people shall be my people, and thy God my God." - Ruth 1:16

"My tears have been my meat day and night, while they continually say unto me, Where is thy God?" - Psalm 42:3

"And Jesus, when he came out, saw much people, and was moved with compassion toward them, because they were as sheep not having a shepherd: and he began to teach them many things."
- Mark 6:34

Scripture Reading: Ruth 1

As often happens with the Bible, I'm seeing something new today in a story that I've read countless times before. God's Word is so rich, so relevant, and so revealing that you can never read it too often. It transcends all the wisdom of this world, and if you learn to rely on it, you'll find that there's never a situation or condition in life that it doesn't address.

So back to this new thing that I've found. It goes back to Naomi, and her going back to Bethlehem. In Ruth 1, life in Moab had been like a shipwreck for Naomi. She had gone there to get away from famine, and had simply found death of another kind (Verses 1-5). Now, having buried a husband and two sons in that God-forsaken land, she is trudging back to Bethlehem (Verses 6-7). She is broken and, by her own admission, bitter (Verse 21).

And here's the new spin (maybe it's not new to you, but it's new to me, anyway). I don't think there's any denying that Naomi was depressed. When I've read this story in the past, I've always pictured Naomi as being too selfless and noble to take her daughters-in-law on the journey with her.

But today, the depths of Naomi's grief really hit me. Pushing those girls away was really a cry for help. Naomi was no great woman of faith (not yet). If she was, she probably wouldn't have ended up in Moab in the first place. Ruth heard the cry for help, and though her faith was new, her compassion was strong. And I believe God blessed her for digging deep to reach Naomi in the pit of her depression.

When Ruth makes her timeless speech of devotion to Naomi (Verses 16-17), she doesn't get a big hug from her mother-in-law or a "thanks, I love you, too". She gets silence (Verse 18). It's almost as if Naomi just gives up and trudges on.

Even once they arrive in Bethlehem, Naomi is dwelling on the past and telling her sad stories to the other women (Verses 19-21). Ruth is the proactive one who goes looking for work and food and by God's grace, finds Boaz along the way (Ruth 2). Her ambition spreads to Naomi in time (by the end of Chapter 3, Naomi is ready to plan Ruth's wedding for her), but in the beginning, Ruth is the one doing all the work to cultivate a new life for them.

I'm going to say something that's going to sound completely compassionless, but it's critical to be honest about this - hurting people can be exhausting.

It's not easy to keep going back for more and reaching back into the pit of depression, and to be even more honest - YOU can't do it alone. Jesus repeatedly took time away to pray, to nap, to get something to eat, and to let His Father rejuvenate Him before He threw Himself back into the fray of needy people that followed Him everywhere (Matthew 14:23, Mark 1:35, Luke 6:12).

But therein lies the key - Jesus kept going back, and He would eventually die for those hurting people (Isaiah 54:5-7, 61:1-2, Mark 10:45). Ruth stuck by Naomi, and today my friend, I'm encouraging you to stick by that hurting someone that God has given you. When hurting people push you away, dig a little deeper. Dig deeper into prayer, deeper into the Word, and deeper into God's wisdom (Hebrews 10:23-25, James 1:5). Ask Him to show you the pain that's behind the hurtful and destructive things that they do and say. Ask Him to help you remember all the times He has dug you out of the muck and the mire (Psalm 42, 66:16-17, 116:1-2).

Hang in there, and hang your hat on God's promises. God Himself is near to the brokenhearted (Psalm 34:18), and wherever He is, you belong there, too. Be a blessing, and you will be blessed. Just ask Mrs. Boaz (Ruth 4:13-14).

YOUR PRESCRIPTION

Ask God to give you the heart of compassion that you need to help someone who is really hurting right now. Ask Him to give you the strength to stick with them through their pain.

SELF EXAMINATION
Is God speaking to you about a problem with your heart?

_____

_____

_____

_____

_____

TREATMENT PLAN
What steps do you need to take to address your heart problem?

_____

_____

_____

_____

_____

Get Real, Get Right

"But he that doeth truth cometh to the light, that his deeds may be made manifest, that they are wrought in God." - John 3:21

"Draw nigh to God, and he will draw nigh to you. Cleanse your hands, ye sinners; and purify your hearts, ye double minded." - James 4:8

"But if we walk in the light, as he is in the light, we have fellowship one with another, and the blood of Jesus Christ his Son cleanseth us from all sin." - I John 1:7

Scripture Reading: John 3

We have a five-year old son, Joey, and one of his favorite games is Hide & Seek. And even though we've pretty much exhausted all of the decent hiding places in our house, he still begs us to play with him over and over. Of course, he'll hide in the same, obvious places each time. And in his five-year old mind, as long as you can't see his face, you can't see him (even though his little feet or his little rear end might be sticking out in plain sight).

I get the impression that Nicodemus played spiritual Hide & Seek. In John 3, Nicodemus comes to Jesus under cover of darkness to ask some of the most critical questions in all of scripture. But although Jesus met Nicodemus where he was, He didn't sugarcoat any of His answers. By day, Nicodemus was a faithful Pharisee and a "ruler of the Jews" (Verse 1), but in the dark, Nicodemus knew that there was a darkness hiding in him.

Actually, I can relate to Nicodemus. There was a time in my life when I didn't want to admit on Sunday who I really was during the rest of the week. I have lived under the illusion that, as long as I could hide the truth, it didn't really matter. But anything that distances you from God absolutely matters.

From a heart that has known hurt, but has also known healing, let me give you a few hard truths to pull you out of your hiding place and into the Light:

1. **Get Real.** No matter who you think you're fooling, you aren't fooling God. When some sin condition - whether of your choosing or someone else's - hinders you from being honest before God, call it what it is. Exercise your free will to free yourself from anything that keeps you from God and His will for your life. (Psalm 51, 66:7-19, 103:1-6, 139:23, Hebrews 4:13)

2. **Get Right.** God forgives. God redeems. God restores. But on the premise of free will, none of these things happen without our repentance. Turn away from your sin, and run from anything and anyone that seeks to drag you back into it. (Joel 2:25, Isaiah 43:1, Romans 2:4, I John 1:9)

3. **Get Into the Light.** In spiritual terms, nothing good grows in darkness, and Satan uses isolation as a breeding ground for a multitude of sins. Ask God to search your heart and shed His light on *all* of your hiding places.

Some may even be news to you. But anything you lay out before Him can be changed and even *used* for His purposes. (John 1:9, 8:12, 11:10, I John 1:7)

4. **Get Into the Word.** All of the wisdom of this world still can't stack up against the truth of God's Word. You can never spend too much time in it, and the more time you do spend, the more God will reveal Himself to you. Most importantly, it will keep your heart and mind away from darkness and filled with the light of His truth. (Psalm 1:1-2, 119:9, 102-104, Jeremiah 33:3, Philippians 4:8, James 1:21)

Nicodemus is mentioned two more times in scripture, and both instances show the impact of his covert conversation with Jesus (John 7:44-52, 19:38-40). In John 7, he would defend Jesus to the agitated Pharisees, diffusing their plans to arrest Him ahead of God's prophetic timetable. And in John 19, he would defy the Jewish leaders by assisting Joseph of Arimathea in the burial of Jesus (another prophecy fulfilled - Deuteronomy 21:23, Isaiah 53:9). It didn't happen overnight, but somewhere along the way, Nicodemus stopped hiding and stepped into the Light.

What about you, my friend? Are their areas of your life that need "His marvelous light" (I Peter 2:9)? No matter what has happened, no matter where you've been or what you've done, even the darkest recesses of your mind, your heart, and your past can be transformed (Romans 12:2) once you get real, get right, and get into the light.

YOUR PRESCRIPTION

What do you have to hide? Be honest with yourself and with God about anything that has come between you, and ask Him to show you anything else that needs to be made right with Him.

SELF EXAMINATION
Is God speaking to you about a problem with your heart?

_____

_____

_____

_____

_____

TREATMENT PLAN
What steps do you need to take to address your heart problem?

_____

_____

_____

_____

_____

Natural Resources

"I have been young, and now am old; yet have I not seen the righteous forsaken, nor his seed begging bread." - Psalm 37:25

"I love the Lord, because he hath heard my voice and my supplications. Because he hath inclined his ear unto me, therefore will I call upon him as long as I live." - Psalm 116:1-2

"When Jesus then lifted up his eyes, and saw a great company come unto him, he saith unto Philip, Whence shall we buy bread, that these may eat? And this he said to prove him: for he himself knew what he would do." - John 6:5-6

Scripture Reading: John 6:1-13

I don't believe I've ever had a full-blown panic attack, but I definitely have had my own special mini version of a panic attack on more than one occasion. It doesn't require professional medical attention - just a few deep breaths and a whole lot of prayer.

You see, when I start to panic, it always seems to stem from two things - my control issues and my inadequacy. The two are a deadly combination. When I look at the things that I want to accomplish, the things that I need to accomplish, and then I stack them up against the natural resources that I have to work with, I start to hyperventilate a little.

In John 6, Jesus poses a question to Philip, and I wouldn't be at all surprised if Philip started to hyperventilate. Jesus had been performing miracles all day long (Matthew 14:14, Mark 6:34, Luke 9:11). Thousands of people are following Jesus as He gets into a boat, and even the Sea of Galilee doesn't deter them (John 6:1-2). As the day continues, they follow Him up a mountainside, and Jesus continues to address both the physical and spiritual needs of the crowd. Now it's late in the day, and they're far from the nearest town. The disciples want to send the people away, but Jesus wants to feed them.

Jesus asks where they can buy bread. It's a question that He doesn't really need answered. He is God in the flesh, and He is the Bread of Life. But Jesus is testing Philip's understanding of *natural* resources versus *supernatural* resources. And even though Philip has had a front row seat for a day of miracles, he is still focused on what is humanly, physically possible. In Verse 7, Philip responds that "two hundred pennyworth" (the equivalent of about half a year's wages) wouldn't feed the people. The task is impossible. The available, natural resources are inadequate.

You know the rest of the story. A little boy's lunch is brought to Jesus. Five thousand are fed (not even counting women and children), everyone eats to their heart's content, and twelve baskets of leftovers are collected.

I don't think it's a coincidence that this is the only miracle of Jesus (other than His resurrection from the grave) that is accounted in each of the four gospels. We often breeze past it, because we've heard it so many times in Sunday School. But while it's a great story for kids, it's a lesson that we as adults need to be reminded of nearly every day.

John 6:7 says that Jesus posed the question to Philip "to prove him: for He himself knew what He would do." Jesus planned to feed the five thousand all along. There was never a doubt that He could and He would. So why do you and I live with doubts that His provision will pick up where our resources leave off?

Multiple challenges factored into this situation - the physical needs of the people, the ongoing work of Jesus' ministry with the disciples, and the resources that were within reach. And in the final analysis, the power and provision of God extended beyond the needs, the inadequacies, and even the expectations of everyone involved (II Corinthians 12:9, Ephesians 3:20, Philippians 4:13, 19).

When you and I panic about our lack of resources, ability, power, control, etc., we completely miss the point. God's contribution is never lacking, and His compassion for our needs is never in question. His resources are limitless. His love knows no bounds. And He knows our needs long before we do (Psalm 16:5, 28:7, 37:25, 55:22, Matthew 7:11, 10:29-31).

Is God posing a question to you today? Is He testing your faith in His supernatural resources? Are your natural resources - be they time, money, or abilities - causing you to have a mini panic attack? Hold on and pray on (Psalm 27:14, 37:34, Matthew 6:33, 7:7). God knows the need (Luke 12:29-31). God has the answer (Proverbs 2:7, 16:1), and His provision is always perfect.

YOUR PRESCRIPTION

Stop worrying and start praying. Whatever need you have, God has the answer. He is your Father, and He longs to help you. Admit that you need His help, and your needs will be met.

SELF EXAMINATION
Is God speaking to you about a problem with your heart?

_____

_____

_____

_____

_____

TREATMENT PLAN
What steps do you need to take to address your heart problem?

_____

_____

_____

_____

_____

Godly Positioning

"Take heed to yourselves, that your heart be not deceived, and ye turn aside, and serve other gods, and worship them." - Deuteronomy 11:16

"Only be thou strong and very courageous, that thou mayest observe to do according to all the law, which Moses my servant commanded thee: turn not from it to the right hand or to the left, that thou mayest prosper withersoever thou goest." - Joshua 1:7

"A prudent man foreseeth the evil, and hideth himself: but the simple pass on, and are punished." - Proverbs 22:3

Scripture Reading: Judges 2

I have a terrible sense of direction - really terrible. I can't tell you how many times I've gone 20 or more miles out of my way in a botched attempt to reach my destination.

But all of that changed with the glorious introduction of GPS (a.k.a., Global Positioning System). Of course, it's man-made and not entirely perfect. But 9 times out of 10, if I listen to the voice, follow its directions, and stay on the path high-lighted on the screen, I get to my destination on time and with no trouble.

It's simple, right? Knowing that my instincts are flawed and my senses are weak, I rely on the most perfect guide I can find, and I follow it to the letter. So why is it so hard in our spiritual lives? We know God's Word is perfect, we know His ways are perfect, and yet, instead of staying right on the path, we find a million different detours, unplanned stops, and the occasional illegal U-turn, forever "recalculating" God's plan for us.

In Judges 2, we see an illegal U-turn in the direction of the Children of Israel. It is a time of victory, prosperity, and eventually, *ingratitude*. Joshua and his leadership team are dying off, and Israel's resolve to obey the Lord is dying along with them. As each tribe moves to claim its inheritance in the Promised Land, compromises abound. Although the Lord had clearly instructed them not to make alliances or to share their world with the Canaanites, they did just that.

In Judges 1 (starting in Verse 25), they allow the Jebusites to stay in the land with the tribe of Benjamin, and one group after another is given an alternative to leaving (meaning that no one who is supposed to leave actually does). The foreign gods never go. The ungodly customs and cultures never go. They all just mix in with the Israelites, constantly watering down their devotion to God, and eventually drowning it out altogether (Judges 2:12-13).

By the second chapter of Judges, God is fed up with their unfaithfulness, and so a sad cycle begins (Judges 2:14). The Children of Israel are oppressed by the Canaanites living among them, and the Promised Land becomes a new "land of affliction" (Verses 15-20). They cry to God for mercy, and because of His covenant with them, He shows mercy, providing a judge to save them (Psalm 124). But even after deliverance, they still refuse to give up the things that violate God's commands, and so they end up right back where they started - having their own stubborn way and living in self-imposed oppression (Deuteronomy 30:8-9, 19-20, Romans 6:17-18).

Are we so different? We question why life is so hard, why God seems so distant, and we wonder why He hasn't done more for us, rarely questioning our own hearts, our actions, and the things in this world that we choose to cling to (Joshua 1:7, Romans 8:6).

I'm here to tell you the hard truth - *in love*. If you really want to know God and His perfect plan for your life, if you want to have peace, when things go your way and even when they don't, *some things have to go* - some things that seem harmless, that seem under your control, and that may have played a comfortable part in your life for a long time. I don't need to tell you what they are, because I would guess that the Holy Spirit has already started to tell you. I'm just here to confirm it.

Check your GPS - that is, the Godly Positioning System that consists of His Word and the Holy Spirit. Listen to His Voice, follow His directions, avoid U-turns, and don't be afraid to leave a few things behind (Psalm 16:11, 119:105, Proverbs 4:18, John 16:13). The final destination will be worth it - He promised.

YOUR PRESCRIPTION

Check your direction and check your baggage. Ask God to show you the road that He has for you, and to show you the things that you should leave behind. Travel light, and travel in the light of His Word.

SELF EXAMINATION
Is God speaking to you about a problem with your heart?

_____

_____

_____

_____

_____

TREATMENT PLAN
What steps do you need to take to address your heart problem?

_____

_____

_____

_____

_____

On the Radar

"For the eyes of the Lord run to and fro throughout the whole earth, to shew himself strong in the behalf of them whose heart is perfect toward him." - II Chronicles 16:9a

"Seek the Lord while he may be found, call ye upon him while he is near: Let the wicked forsake his way, and the unrighteous man his thoughts: and let him return unto the Lord, and he will have mercy upon him; and to our God, for he will abundantly pardon." - Isaiah 55:6-7

"Run ye to and fro through the streets of Jerusalem, and see now, and know, and seek in the broad places thereof, if ye can find a man, if there be any that executeth judgment, that seeketh the truth; and I will pardon it."
- Jeremiah 5:1

Scripture Reading: II Chronicles 15; Jeremiah 5

I t's true we never know what a day holds. The past week proved that to me, and I never even saw it coming. In the space of just three days, life was good, then life was bad, then life was really bad, then unbelievably bad, and then (by God's grace), life was great.

There is a place that each of us needs to be, and that place is, as the old hymn says, "near to the heart of God". And I'll tell you why. In this fallen world, an endless list of things can shake your world to the core without warning. There are hurts and challenges and unexpected turns that no amount of life experience can prepare you for, and when they hit, I promise that you'll want your need to be blinking right in the middle of God's radar.

II Chronicles 15 and Jeremiah 5 both give us a glimpse of God's radar in action. Both chapters recount a period in the history of the Kingdom of Judah. In II Chronicles 15, we meet King Asa, who for 35 years was on God's radar for all the right reasons. He was one of those rare kings who tried to pull Judah *away* from worshipping other gods - even removing his own mother from power because of her idolatry.

But in II Chronicles 16, Asa would make a critical mistake. After decades of peace and blessing from the hand of God, Judah was under threat from the northern tribes of Israel and their new king. Asa's response is pretty insulting to the God that has prospered him to this point. He puts together a protection payment, consisting of gold and silver from the king's treasury, as well as (don't miss this) the House of the Lord. He then gives this payment of protection to the king of Syria. This is a bad idea on so many levels that I can't even take the time to fully explain it. But you probably don't need me to.

In II Chronicles 16:9, God reveals His heart to Asa. God's eyes are forever searching for hearts that are turned in His direction. They "run to and fro" looking for the faithful, for everyday, ordinary people seeking to do God's will. God's desire is to find us seeking Him, in the good times and bad, so that whatever our need, He can show Himself faithful to us.

Fast-forward to Jeremiah 5. The eyes of the Lord are again searching, looking for any sign of repentance, any desire to return to Him, on the part of Judah. Sadly, He finds nothing, and again, Judah is on God's radar in a bad way. While He wants to pardon, wants to bless, wants to be found, His holy nature is forced to keep His covenant - blessings for obedience, curses for disobedience (Deuteronomy 30:19). Stubborn Judah offers no obedience and no repentance, and Babylon is poised to serve as God's justice against their rebellion (Psalm 137:1, Jeremiah 20:4).

You and I are on God's radar today, but whether we're on it for the right reason or the wrong reason is up to us. When God's eyes search to and fro, I want Him to find me faithful. I want to and I *need to* be able to call on Him in the day of trouble, with a pure heart (Psalm 50:15, 86:7, 116:2, Matthew 5:8, Hebrews 10:21-23).

God is good, and the offer of forgiveness is always on the table. But make no mistake about it - God's best blessings, God's greatest deliverance, and His strong arm are extended to those who are reaching up to Him (II Samuel 22:4, Jeremiah 29:13, Zephaniah 3:9, James 4:8). And while salvation is forever, you never want to be on His radar for the wrong reason.

Tribulation will come. Life will sucker-punch you when you least expect it. But there is a Healer, there is a Deliverer, there is a God Who is mighty to save. Set your sights on Him, and you'll be in His sights when you need it most.

YOUR PRESCRIPTION

Seek God - every day, in every way you can. Don't let distraction, boredom, bitterness, or pride keep you from getting on His radar for the right reasons. He is searching for the faithful right now. Let Him find you faithful, and you will find Him.

SELF EXAMINATION

Is God speaking to you about a problem with your heart?

_____

_____

_____

_____

_____

TREATMENT PLAN

What steps do you need to take to address your heart problem?

_____

_____

_____

_____

_____

Attitude Adjustments

"Search me, O God, and know my heart: try me, and know my thoughts: And see if there be any wicked way in me, and lead me in the way everlasting." - Psalm 139:23-24

"Put on therefore, as the elect of God, holy and beloved, bowels of mercies, kindness, humbleness of mind, meekness, longsuffering; Forbearing one another, and forgiving one another, if any man have a quarrel against any: even as Christ forgave you, so also do ye."
- Colossians 3:12-13

Scripture Reading: Colossians 3

We're working on "sharing" in my house. As the mother of a 5-year old, I often have to intervene in matters of sharing toys, taking turns, and other basic attitude adjustments. And though he needs frequent adjustments, when my 5-year old gets it right, it makes me smile.

Maybe I'm more like a 5-year old than I realize. I'm often convicted of the fact that, in my supposedly "grown-up" life, my attitude needs frequent (even moment-by-moment) adjustment.

As Christians, we often convince ourselves that because we've cleaned up our act, we are clean before God. But in Colossians 3, Paul contends that attitudes are the root of our actions. And just like you can pull a weed, and not kill it if you haven't pulled up the root, if you clean up your act without cleaning up your attitudes, the act will only last for so long (Proverbs 4:23).

In Verses 1-4, we are told that since we are risen in Christ, we should live in Christ. That makes sense. I can absolutely get on board with that idea. As we move into Verse 5, Paul starts to list the obvious, outward sins that need to go - immorality, lust, greed, and the actions that easily define a life lived outside of the will of God. But in Verse 8, he starts to dig deeper, getting into everyday thoughts and attitudes, which can spring up even in the cleanest of lives - things like anger, lying, and corrupt communication, in general. The real challenge starts here.

In Verse 10, he points out that the Christian life is all about being the "new man" or the "new creature" (II Corinthians 5:17). And it not only involves a new attitude towards God, but a new attitude towards others as well. As we live in the abundance of His mercy, we learn to extend mercy, to forgive and forbear (Verses 12-15, Micah 6:8, Matthew 5:7, Romans 12:10, Ephesians 4:32). Paul then gives some practical ways to maintain our new attitude. Now we're getting somewhere. Psalms, hymns, spiritual songs - I love all of that, and I truly believe that to spiritually be in your right mind, you need to fill your mind with the right stuff (Verse 16).

And now that Paul has our attention on the attitudes and the adjustment, he goes for the application. Verses 18-22 drive it home - literally. It's not just about walking around in my little spiritual bubble, singing hymns and thanking God for the stuff I like. It's about test-driving my new attitude over and over, in the very real and sometimes messy moment-by-moment interactions with my spouse, my kids, and all of the other people in my life that are supposed to be more important than me (which, according to my Bible, is everyone). And when my attitude fails the test (as it often does), I need to get back in the Word and ask God to help me make *more* adjustments, so that the next test-drive goes a little more smoothly and gives Him a lot more glory.

My question to you today - where are *you* in this process? Are you deliberately, intentionally, and prayerfully adjusting the attitudes in your heart on a daily basis? Surface cleanup is temporary at best. Deep, heart-cleaning attitude adjustments have eternal value and glorify God better (Romans 12:2, II Corinthians 10:5). In short, they make God *smile* (Psalm 37:23-24).

Today, I'm working on being less like a 5-year old, and more like Jesus, who humbled Himself to die the death that I deserved (Philippians 2:7-9). He put me before Himself, so I will deliberately and prayerfully adjust my attitude to put *Him* first, *others* second, and *myself* last.

And when the 5-year old in me gets the best of me, and I feel my attitude failing, I'll go back to the cross for another helping of mercy (Hebrews 4:15-16), so I can work on sharing that mercy all over again.

YOUR PRESCRIPTION

Work on your sharing. Share Christ in the everyday by sharing His mercy with those around you. Ask Him to adjust your attitude so that He can shine through you to someone who needs Him.

SELF EXAMINATION
Is God speaking to you about a problem with your heart?

_____

_____

_____

_____

_____

TREATMENT PLAN
What steps do you need to take to address your heart problem?

_____

_____

_____

_____

_____

A Different Light

"And the glory of the Lord shall be revealed, and all flesh shall see it together: for the mouth of the Lord hath spoken it...The grass withereth, the flower fadeth: but the word of our God shall stand for ever...Hast thou not known? hast thou not heard, that the everlasting God, the Lord, the Creator of the ends of the earth, fainteth not, neither is weary? there is no searching of his understanding." - Isaiah 40:5, 8, 28

"And their eyes were opened, and they knew him; and he vanished out of their sight. And they said one to another, Did not our heart burn within us, while he talked with us by the way, and while he opened to us the scriptures?" - Luke 24:31-32

Scripture Reading: Luke 24:13-32

It's funny. When I was younger, I wanted to be a journalist. In my mind, I had this romanticized idea of the glamorous and exciting life of a news reporter. Some thirty years later, my perspective on the news is quite different. I'm struck not only by the endless talk of tragedy, but by the sad realization of how much trouble the world is in, when left in human hands.

In Luke 24, Jesus' followers are still reeling from His death at the hands of their local leaders. Mary Magdalene and the women have returned from His grave with stories of angels and an empty tomb, but the reality of the resurrection hasn't taken hold yet. Verse 11 basically tells us that the men thought the women were crazy ("their words seemed to them as idle tales"), and although none of them had an explanation for the empty tomb, none of them believed that Jesus could actually have risen from the dead, either.

In Verse 12, Peter goes to the tomb to see for himself, but he still can't wrap his head around what's happened. Two nameless followers of Jesus leave Jerusalem and set out for the village of Emmaus (about 7 miles away). Not surprisingly, they are troubled by the events of recent days. The cause that they had built their lives around now seems hopeless, and their pain seems pointless. As they talk of the tragedy, a stranger joins in (Verses 15-16). He appears to be completely unaware of the local news, and as they fill Him in, they can only talk about the trouble wrought by human hands (Verse 20).

But in Verse 25, Jesus starts to explain the same events in a completely different light. He takes their 6 o'clock news account and puts it in the context of scripture, prophecy, and God's plan. For these two disciples, it is an eye-opening experience, as their sorrow is intertwined with sovereignty. The pain of the crucifixion doesn't go away, but it loses its senselessness in the light of God's sovereign plan and prophecy fulfilled. This sad story is not simply the work of human hands - it is a stitch in time, as the Unseen Hand of God weaves His purpose through even the most horrible of events. And because those are the same Hands that first formed the world, and will one day make all things new again, the story is not over (Genesis 50:20, Job 19:25, Psalm 18:2, 25:20, 90:2, Revelation 21:5). It does not end on a hopeless and senseless note, but with a glorious and deliberate purpose.

In Verse 31, they realize that Jesus Himself has been walking and talking with them all this time. It suddenly all clicks. *He is alive.* The purpose of His death was to rise again. The pain was all part of the prophecy (Isaiah 53, I Corinthians 15:3-4). Human hands were never really in control here. The Unseen Hand of God ordained and executed it all, and their hearts burned with a new understanding of Him (Isaiah 40).

Now, take *your* tragedy. You think you can't make sense of it, and I dare say you never will. In human hands, the hurts of this life are pointless, senseless, and cruel. But hold your hurts up to the light of scripture, and your heart will burn with a renewed understanding (Psalm 93:1, 119:71, Isaiah 43:2, Luke 24:32). I'm not saying you'll have all the answers. I'm not saying the pain will go away, but mix a little sovereignty in with your sorrow, and you'll see that the story's not over yet.

If you're walking a difficult road today, ask Jesus to meet you where you are. But don't be surprised to find that He's already there, walking right beside you, and just waiting to give you a new understanding of His work in your life. Human hands are not in control here (Psalm 27:1, 56:11, Proverbs 10:22, Zephaniah 3:17). Get a hold of the Unseen Hand, and see your world in a different light.

YOUR PRESCRIPTION

Do not settle for a 6 o'clock news perspective of the events in your life. Get into God's Word, and get His perspective on the things that are happening to you. He is your hope. He is in control. And He is not finished with you yet.

SELF EXAMINATION

Is God speaking to you about a problem with your heart?

_____

_____

_____

_____

_____

TREATMENT PLAN

What steps do you need to take to address your heart problem?

_____

_____

_____

_____

Behind the Bread

"But thou shalt remember the Lord thy God: for it is he that giveth thee power to get wealth, that he may establish his covenant which he sware unto thy fathers, as it is this day."
                                                    - Deuteronomy 8:18

"But who am I, and what is my people, that we should be able to offer so willingly after this sort? for all things come of thee, and of thine own have we given thee." - I Chronicles 29:14

"And said, Naked came I out of my mother's womb, and naked shall I return thither: the Lord gave, and the Lord hath taken away; blessed be the name of the Lord." - Job 1:21

Scripture Reading: Deuteronomy 8; I Chronicles 29:1-16

I have a confession to make - I like my stuff. I'm the kind of girl who has a purse to go with every pair of shoes, and as my husband will tell you, I have way too many shoes. I've had to scale back my tastes in recent years, as the Lord's been teaching me to live abundantly on a less-than-abundant budget, but I still have my little stockpile of stuff that I love.

I recently gave away some of my precious stuff, and I'm ashamed to admit, it was a little hard. For just a moment, I wondered if I could do without it. Maybe I was being too hasty. Maybe I needed to keep my stuff for myself a little longer. I shouldn't have been surprised to find that God quickly replaced my stuff in wonderful and unexpected ways. My feeble attempt to be a blessing to someone else resulted in way more blessings than I deserved.

How soon we forget where all our stuff comes from (Ecclesiastes 3:13, Luke 12:20, James 1:17). In Deuteronomy 8, Moses is basically holding a review class with the Children of Israel. His time as their leader is winding down, and he is reminding them of the laws God had given them, as well as the blessings attached to obedience.

In Verse 3, he reminds them of the hunger that threatened them in the wilderness, and the provision of God that saved them - manna. And he lets them in on a little secret - both the hunger *and* the manna were sent by God, so that they could realize their need for Him and then experience His goodness (Psalm 42:8, 63:3, 119:67, 71, Lamentations 3:19-26).

In Verses 7-10, Moses tells the people that they are about to experience the goodness of God in a new way. In the Promised Land, they will eat until they are full, and they will have a variety of blessings to enjoy, but he adds another reminder. Abundance is coming, and in a fallen world, abundance is frequently followed by *arrogance*. In Verses 17-18, Moses tells them to never forget the manna, never let their successes go to their head, and never forget *Who* is behind the bread.

Fast-forward to the final days of King David. In I Chronicles 29, David is passing the reigns of His kingdom to Solomon, along with a precious stockpile. For years, David has been setting aside resources to build the temple. Although the task of building is saved for his son, David has led the people in giving all the materials required for the project, and it's some pretty lavish stuff - gold, silver, and precious stones (Verses 3-8). But

David puts the whole project into perspective in Verses 12-16, as He acknowledges the One behind the bread. I love these words, and I hope to remember them every time I think I am making a sacrifice for God, "Of thine own have we given thee."

We cling so tightly to our stuff, and we cling to the illusion that we have somehow acquired it on our own. But make no mistake about it, God is *always* the One behind the bread. It was true in Moses' day, it was true in David's day, and it's true every day of our lives.

Hold loosely to the stuff of life. And don't get too wrapped up in the accumulation of earthly things. And when you have an abundance of earthly things, give them away and give God the credit, so that someone else can be drawn to the God who gave you those things in the first place. Everything belongs to Him, so don't ever worry that you'll go without (Psalm 24:1, Isaiah 55:1-2, Matthew 6:8, 32). He knows your need, and far greater treasure awaits in the presence of the One behind the bread (Matthew 6:19-21).

YOUR PRESCRIPTION

Give it away. Take something from your abundance (and trust me, with God you always have some kind of abundance) and give it to someone else in the name of Jesus. Ask God to give you an opportunity to bless someone with the blessings He's given you.

SELF EXAMINATION
Is God speaking to you about a problem with your heart?

_____

_____

_____

_____

_____

TREATMENT PLAN
What steps do you need to take to address your heart problem?

_____

_____

_____

_____

_____

Flirting with Fire

"Stolen waters are sweet, and bread eaten in secret is pleasant. But he knoweth not that the dead are there; and that her guests are in the depths of hell." - Proverbs 9:17-18

"Let no man say when he is tempted, I am tempted of God: for God cannot be tempted with evil, neither tempteth he any man: But every man is tempted, when he is drawn away of his own lust, and enticed." - James 1:13

Scripture Reading: Proverbs 5

There's a sad irony in life. Our successes often rise upon the failures of others. In order for someone to win, someone else has to lose. It happened in our salvation. For us to live, Christ had to die (Isaiah 53:5, 10, Romans 6:23). It is also true in learning. Our human nature seems to learn better from the sad stories of others than from the simple truths of God's Word.

Maybe that's why Solomon wove so many sad stories of the "adulterous woman" into the simple truths of Proverbs. She occupies a lot of real estate in Solomon's book of wisdom. Just off the top of my head, she is mentioned in Proverbs 5, 7, 8, 9, and 20 - nothing to sneeze at. And I think she points to another subject that we shouldn't sneeze at - the simple concept of *flirting with fire*.

It runs rampant, even in some Christian circles. We don't like to talk about it, but we're forced to face it every time another Christian marriage is lost to adultery. We hate to admit it, but it's easy to feed your ego and fulfill unmet needs with the attention of the wrong person. The world will certainly understand, but it is *not* God's way.

You can tell yourself that flirting is harmless, but once you start looking in the wrong direction for affection, there are always tempters and temptresses who invite you to come just a little bit closer to the fire (Proverbs 6:13-14). They make the slippery slope of compromise look like a slide at the playground, but make no mistake, there's nothing but regret and heartache waiting at the bottom of that slide.

Please don't think I'm here to condemn. Outside of the grace of God, I would be the first to go down in flames (literally). I'm here to plead with you to understand the irony of Solomon. He writes from the wrong side, the tragic side of this issue. He was the man to whom God gave the greatest portion of wisdom (I Kings 3, 4:29-32), and yet he was the man who failed most miserably in this area (I Kings 11:3-4), and he had 300 wives and 700 concubines to prove it.

And this brings me to the most important point. You can know what God's Word says, and you can have all the wisdom in the world, but if God doesn't really have your heart, then your heart will be up for grabs to the flirts of this world (Psalm 119:11, Matthew 5:28, 7:15-17, 15:8, 23:27, Luke 16:15).

Solomon didn't just end up with *more* women; he ended up with *less* God. The Bible clearly tells us that his wives turned his heart from the Lord. They certainly pulled him closer to the fire, persuading him to worship their gods. And eventually, the builder of God's temple was building temples for idols such as the Ammonite god, Molech (I Kings 11:6-7), and this deplorable idol worship would stay with Israel for generations to come (Jeremiah 32:34-35). And just as the fires of Molech killed countless innocent children, countless modern-day families are destroyed by affairs and immorality that started from tiny, unassuming sparks of flirtation. *Don't go there.*

Again, I'm only here to plead with you. Guard your heart (Proverbs 4:23). Guard the sanctity of marriage. Guard the morality and the purity of the Church. Guard your relationship with God and the other relationships that He has blessed you with. Satan is gunning for all of those things (I Peter 5:8).

If you are a wife, be the wife that your husband needs (Proverbs 31:10-12, Ephesians 5:21-22). If you are single, wait on God's man for you, in God's timing (Jeremiah 29:11). And by God's grace, be the beauty that rises from the ashes and the success that learns from the failure of others (Isaiah 61:3). And wherever you are, be the kind of gracious and godly woman that discourages flirting with fire.

YOUR PRESCRIPTION

Check your heart. Make sure that all of your affections are in the right place, and if your heart is wandering, confess it to God. Ask Him to help you to love Him more than anyone else, and the rest of your affections will fall back into line.

SELF EXAMINATION
Is God speaking to you about a problem with your heart?

_____

_____

_____

_____

_____

TREATMENT PLAN
What steps do you need to take to address your heart problem?

_____

_____

_____

_____

_____

TLC

"One thing have I desired of the Lord, that will I seek after; that I may dwell in the house of the Lord all the days of my life, to behold the beauty of the Lord, and to enquire in his temple."
- Psalm 27:4

"O God, thou art my God; early will I seek thee: my soul thirsteth for thee, my flesh longeth for thee in a dry and thirsty land, where no water is; To see thy power and thy glory, so as I have seen thee in the sanctuary." - Psalm 63:1-2

"Walk in wisdom toward them that are without, redeeming the time. Let your speech be always with grace, seasoned with salt, that ye may know how ye ought to answer every man."
- Colossians 4:5-6

Scripture Reading: Psalm 27

There was a day not long ago, when I couldn't wait to get to church, and I'll tell you why. Honestly, I needed a little TLC (tender loving care). The week had been long, my heart was heavy, and my feeble prayers didn't feel like enough.

As soon as I stepped into the sanctuary, I started scanning the room for a certain friend of mine. She hugs me every time she sees me - the kind of heartfelt bear hug where you can almost feel her trying to transfer some of her own strength to you. She never fails to ask me how I'm doing, and she's not looking for a canned answer of five words or less - she's looking for raw specifics and unvarnished truth. And if I ask her to pray for something, she writes it down on a piece of paper that she keeps in her Bible. She's one of the people that has made church a refuge for me. She makes it feel like home.

I have another friend who I also love dearly, but frankly, this one worries me. She needs a little TLC, but she doesn't seem to know where to find it. She's had a lot of heartache in her life in recent years, and circumstances have piled up between her and God. She doesn't see church as a refuge. She doesn't even feel at home there anymore. Personal loss combined with politics and pettiness has sent her running away from church, and Sunday is becoming more and more like another Saturday.

In Psalm 27, David acknowledges that "the house of the Lord" feels like home to him. In Verse 4, he says that his greatest desire, his lifelong wish, is to be in God's temple and to seek God. It's the only place he feels safe (Verse 5), the only place he feels loved (Verse 10), and the only place that gives him hope (Verse 13).

If anyone needed a little TLC, it was David. He was no stranger to personal loss, politics, or pettiness. It is estimated that he spent 13 years running from Saul (I Samuel 24:8-13) and nearly 10 years fending off his son Absalom's treason (II Samuel 15:13-14), and he understood many of the heartaches of life in a fallen world. He knew what it was like to lose a marriage (I Samuel 25:44). He knew what it was like to lose a child (II Samuel 12:18). He knew what it was like to fail (II Samuel 12:7-10), and to have your nearest and dearest turn on you (Psalm 69:4-8).

But all these things didn't drive David away from God; they drove him to God and to His house (Psalm 84:9-11, 100, 122:1).

There he praised the God who was his confidence in the chaos, his shelter in the storm, and the Rock of his salvation.

Folks, it should be the same for us. As the world gets crazier, we should pull God closer (Isaiah 55:6, Matthew 11:28-30, Ephesians 5:15-17). If this world is not your home, then the closest thing to a home that you can hope to have in this world is the house of the Lord. Make yourself at home there and seek answers in God's presence and in His Word.

The Lord's house is meant to be a hospital for sin-sick souls (Isaiah 61:1-3, Mark 2:17). Make church your personal refuge, and go out of your way to make it a refuge for someone else (Colossians 3:11-13, 4:5-6, Hebrews 10: 24-25, Jude 21-23). God never turns away anyone who comes to Him with a broken heart, and may God forgive us if we trample over the broken hearts entrusted to us.

May everyone who walks into the house of the Lord be able to feel His love through the people who claim to be His own. And may *The Love of Christ* be the TLC that we give to a lost and dying world.

YOUR PRESCRIPTION

The next time you go to church, go out of your way to make someone else glad they came. Step out of your pew and your comfort zone to give TLC (The Love of Christ) to someone who needs it. God will bless you for it.

SELF EXAMINATION
Is God speaking to you about a problem with your heart?

_____

_____

_____

_____

_____

TREATMENT PLAN
What steps do you need to take to address your heart problem?

_____

_____

_____

_____

_____

The Last Supper

"For thus saith the Lord God of Israel, The barrel of meal shall not waste, neither shall the cruse of oil fail, until the day that the Lord sendeth rain upon the earth. And she went and did according to the saying of Elijah: and she, and he, and her house, did eat many days."
— I Kings 17:14-15

"Fear thou not; for I am with thee: be not dismayed; for I am thy God: I will strengthen thee; yea, I will help thee; yea, I will uphold thee with the right hand of my righteousness."
— Isaiah 41:10

"And he that taketh not his cross, and followeth after me, is not worthy of me. He that findeth his life shall lose it: and he that loseth his life for my sake shall find it." — Matthew 10:38-39

Scripture Reading: I Kings 17:7-24

A friend of mine once said to me, "I don't live to eat. I eat to live." I was baffled by those words and convicted at the same time. I come from a family where food was always the star of the show. It was the cure for whatever ailed you, the prize to be won, and an expression of love.

You can imagine my surprise when I ended up with a child who only "eats to live". My five-year old has no internal clock when it comes to meals (while you could set your watch by *my* appetite). Eating isn't anywhere near the top of his priority list, and in his mind, meals interfere with his play time. And although he is super active and more athletic than anyone with my DNA has a right to be, I'm forever worried that he doesn't eat enough.

But in I Kings 17, the widow at Zarephath had *real* reason to worry about her son. She lived in the northern kingdom of Israel, where Ahab and Jezebel ruled.

Although his forefathers had been pretty evil, Ahab had outdone them all (I Kings 16:30-33). As punishment, God had sent the prophet Elijah to declare a drought - no rain until further notice from God. And here's how that boiled down to a humble widow and her little boy: a couple of sticks for a fire, a handful of flour and a few drops of oil. We have our last supper, and then we wait to die.

Enter Elijah. In Verses 10 and 11, he makes two simple requests - a little water and a bit of bread. But make no mistake, these are precious commodities in uncertain times. She was on her way to get Elijah his drink of water, but the request for bread forced her hand. She only had one meal left, and barely a meal at that. She had a son, and she knew that their time was short.

This man was asking a lot. And then he asks a little more.

In Verse 13, Elijah tells her to proceed with her plan, BUT she must feed *him* first. The promise follows in Verse 14 - the flour and oil will never run out for the duration of the drought. But the promise requires specific obedience - obedience that puts the man of God before her, and even before her son.

As a mom, I find this to be a tall order. With the resources she had, she could eke out a few more days with her boy. If she wanted God's help, she had to give up all that she had, the last of her own resources, and trust a promise. Elijah didn't come rolling up with a visible supply of blessings for this woman - there were no sacks of flour or vats of oil in view. There was just a promise that required a blind leap of faith on her part.

And it's often that way with us. God's promises don't always have specific solutions, timelines, and a grocery list of blessings attached. Sometimes, they require a leap of faith, a little sacrifice, and trading our "sure thing" for God's "better thing" (Hebrews 11:40).

Is God asking you to give up a sure thing today, in order to realize His plan for you? I am guessing that you have considerably more than a handful of flour to your name, and I am sure you know that everything you have to your name came from the God Who knows both your name and your need (Matthew 7:11, Philippians 4:19, James 1:17).

Trust Him (Psalm 20:7, Proverbs 3:5-6, Jeremiah 17:7-8). **Obey Him** - even when it doesn't make sense, even when it seems that obedience will make things worse. God's plan may be beyond your understanding now, but His best blessings go hand-in-hand with your obedience (Deuteronomy 5:33, Matthew 4:4, 6:33, Luke 9:23, 11:28, John 14:23).

Get it through your head. God's kingdom works differently - losing is winning, dying is living, least is greatest, and last is first. This widow's *last* supper turned out to be the *first* supper of the rest of her life, and she learned that the blessings never run out - when you trust and obey.

YOUR PRESCRIPTION

Trust His promises. If you're clinging to a sure thing and God is telling you to let go, listen to Him. He is sovereign, He owns the cattle on a thousand hills, and He loves you. You'll never give up anything for Him that He can't replace tenfold.

SELF EXAMINATION
Is God speaking to you about a problem with your heart?

_____

_____

_____

_____

_____

TREATMENT PLAN
What steps do you need to take to address your heart problem?

_____

_____

_____

_____

_____

Comfort Food

*"Let Pharaoh do this, and let him appoint offi-
cers over the land, and take up the fifth part of
the land of Egypt in the seven plenteous years...
And that food shall be for store to the land
against the seven years of famine, which shall
be in the land of Egypt; that the land perish not
through the famine." - Genesis 41:34, 36*

*"And I said, This is my infirmity: but I will
remember the years of the right hand of the
most High. I will remember the works of the
Lord: surely I will remember thy wonders of old.
I will meditate also of all thy work, and talk of
thy doings." - Psalm 77:10-12*

*"Unless thy law had been my delights, I should
then have perished in mine affliction. I will
never forget thy precepts: for with them thou
hast quickened me." - Psalm 119:92-93*

Scripture Reading: Genesis 41:14-57

Today, my thoughts are with a distant but dear friend of
mine who recently suffered an unimaginable loss. When
I first heard that this bright and beautiful young woman had
lost her baby girl in a tragic accident, I was sick to my stomach

with grief for her. I can't even fathom where this loss will take her - the dark days and the oceans of tears that lie ahead. But one thing gives me hope - I know this girl, and I know that she has spent her lifetime storing up faith to get her through this famine. And I want to encourage you do to do the same.

In Genesis 41, Joseph has finally been remembered, and his prison stint is about to end. Pharaoh has had a dream, and now he needs answers. Of course, the court magicians are useless (Genesis 41:7-8), but Pharaoh's dilemma reminds his cupbearer of his own prison stint a few years earlier. He immediately refers Joseph (Verses 9-13), who immediately refers Pharaoh to the One True God (Verse 16). And by God's grace, Joseph not only provides the interpretation of the dream, but the intervention required to survive the famine to come.

The first seven years will be fantastic, with plenty of food for all. The next seven years will be famine - famine so severe that it will wipe out every last memory of the good years. The solution: it's all about saving and storing. Use the time of plenty to prepare for the time of poverty. It makes perfect sense, and Joseph is the perfect man for the job. Pharaoh appoints him and Joseph goes to work, setting aside 20% of the harvest in storage for the lean years (Verse 34).

Joseph's little savings plan is a complete game-changer. The famine still comes with seven years of little to no harvest, but Egypt is ready for it. They sustain their own with the stored-up crops and even serve as a food pantry for the entire region (Genesis 42:1-2), eventually providing food for Joseph's own long-lost family (Genesis 45:4-6, 50:20).

We talk about saving for a rainy day. We put money in savings accounts and 401k's. We buy insurance, and when the local weather man scares us enough, we run out to pick up bread and milk and bottled water, and maybe even a generator. But let me tell you, it is every bit as important - no, far *more* important - that you prep for a famine of *faith* (Psalm 59:16, 124, Ephesians 5:15-17).

Jesus Himself reinforced this concept in the parable of the wise man and the foolish man (Matthew 7:24-27). His imagery really hits home, "And the rain descended, and the floods came, and the winds blew, and beat upon that house..."

A crisis of faith is like that. Something terrible happens, maybe a whole series of terrible things happen, but the effect is the same. You feel beaten down. You feel hit from all sides. And the storm clouds can block your view of God's hand in your life.

And that's why you need a house built on the Rock, and a storehouse of faith - the scriptures you've read (Psalm 1:1-3, 119:11), the prayers you've prayed (Psalm 34:4, 142:5), the blessings you count (Lamentations 3:20-23) and the friends you've made (Proverbs 17:17). Those are the things that will sustain you until the clouds start to break up and God's presence shines brightly in your storm.

Today, I don't have answers. I can't begin to unravel the mysteries of God's sovereign plan. Storms will beat on us and famines will starve our faith, but God's promises and God's goodness will outlast them all. If today is a day of peace and plenty for you, then take the time to fill up on the comfort food of God's Word. Store it up for a rainy day, a dry day, and everything in between.

YOUR PRESCRIPTION

Spend some time filling your storehouse. Seek to spend a little more time in the Word and a little more time in prayer. The more time you spend with God in the sunshine, the easier it will be to find Him in the storm.

SELF EXAMINATION
Is God speaking to you about a problem with your heart?

_____

_____

_____

_____

_____

TREATMENT PLAN
What steps do you need to take to address your heart problem?

_____

_____

_____

_____

_____

A Place for Everything

*"Then the Lord answered Job out of the whirl-
wind, and said, Who is this that darkeneth
counsel by words without knowledge?...Where
wast thou when I laid the foundations of the
earth? declare, if thou hast understanding."*
- Job 38:1-2, 4

*"Then Job answered the Lord, and said, Behold,
I am vile; what shall I answer thee? I will lay
mine hand upon my mouth." - Job 40:3-4*

*"When I consider thy heavens, the work of thy
fingers, the moon and the stars, which thou hast
ordained; What is man, that thou art mindful of
him? and the son of man, that thou visitest him?"*
- Psalm 8:3-4

Scripture Reading: Job 38

Today, my God is so big. Actually, He's big, and amazing,
and awesome, and completely beyond my comprehension
every day. But today, I am keenly aware of Who He is, and if
there's a place for everything, then I am happy to report that I
have been put in mine.

You see, I just returned from a few days in Niagara Falls, Canada. Growing up in the Buffalo area, I've been there many times. My dad even worked as a U.S. Customs Inspector at the Peace Bridge (his summer job during his early teaching years), so we did plenty of day trips to Niagara Falls. But this time was different. My husband wisely insisted that we get as close to the water as possible. There are plenty of man-made attractions in a hyper-developed tourist area like the Falls (modern man is still forever trying to out-build God's creation and rebuild the Tower of Babel). But God's majesty in those incredible water-falls still outshines all the tinsel that man has tried to hang on that world wonder (Psalm 19:1, Romans 1:20, Revelation 4:11).

It made me feel small. To be reminded of how BIG He is - to stand on a boat, then in a cave, then on a boardwalk, all in the shadow of those mighty, thundering waters - made me feel unbelievably, infinitesimally small, and dare I say, a little help-less. It was definitely a "How Great Thou Art" moment. I'll say it again: it put me in my place.

In Job 38, God puts Job in his place. This chapter (and the one after it) are filled with images that simply boggle the mind. Job seems to be nearing his breaking point. He has lost his ten children, his wealth and his health, all by the unseen and unbridled hand of Satan (remember, God said Satan could take everything but Job's life in Job 2:6). His wife has turned on him, and as if that wasn't enough, his three closest "friends" spend a good 30 chapters trying to verbally beat a confession out of Job (Job 19:2-3). Convinced that Job must have something to hide (why else would God allow trouble?), they are relentless.

But after they have run their mouths for what had to have been days, God finally steps in to set the record straight. He is sovereign. He doesn't owe man an explanation, and even if He chose to give one, we could never wrap our feeble and finite minds around it (Psalm 135:6, Job 38:4, 10, 12, Isaiah 45:9-12, Daniel 4:35, Ephesians 3:20).

In our pride, we desperately crave understanding. We have the audacity to think that sorting out the mysteries of creation puts us in league with the Creator. We think that making money, maintaining our own little castles, and building our own little kingdoms in our own little power puts us in league with the King of Kings. We think that our rags of human righteousness put us in league with a perfect and holy God, and we torture ourselves thinking that we have to figure our way out of the problems that only He can fix.

Know your place and embrace it. He is everything, and we are nothing, but because He first loved us, we can have everything through the righteousness of His Son (I John 3:1, 4:18-19). He is great and mighty and awesome, and we are weak and small, but because He is so great, our problems, our needs, and our fears all shrink in His presence (Psalm 27:1, Isaiah 41:10). That worry that keeps you up at night is a small thing to Him. He cares, but He is nowhere near overwhelmed.

It's true - there *is* a place for everything. God's place is on the throne of our lives. Our place is on our knees. And the place for everything that ails us is at the foot of the cross. Be amazed at all He is. Be humbled by all you are not. Give God the glory, and give Him His rightful place.

YOUR PRESCRIPTION

Does God have His rightful place in your life? Let creation remind you of His awesomeness and put you in your place. Stop controlling, stop questioning, and start humbling yourself before the great and mighty God Who loves you.

SELF EXAMINATION
Is God speaking to you about a problem with your heart?

_____

_____

_____

_____

_____

TREATMENT PLAN
What steps do you need to take to address your heart problem?

_____

_____

_____

_____

_____

Where Faith Lives

"And he could there do no mighty work, save that he laid his hands upon a few sick folk, and healed them. And he marvelled because of their unbelief." - Mark 6:5-6a

"And straightway the father of the child cried out, and said with tears, Lord, I believe; help thou mine unbelief." - Mark 9:24

"And I say unto you, Ask, and it shall be given you; seek, and ye shall find; knock, and it shall be opened unto you. For every one that asketh receiveth; and he that seeketh findeth; and to him that knocketh it shall be opened."
- Luke 11:9-10

Scripture Reading: Mark 6:1-6

I come from a long line of exceptionally stubborn people, and we have our family legends to back it up. When my great aunt stubbornly insisted that she was quitting high school a year before graduation, my great uncle (her older brother) picked her up and physically carried her into school with equal stubbornness.

While I tend to be one of the more easygoing personalities in my family, I'm ashamed to say that I can be hard-headed when it comes to hope. I want to believe that things can change, that people can change - and most importantly, that God changes things - but there are times when I've just seen too much, and what I have seen makes faith seem like folly.

Time and time again, I catch myself giving up on someone, tired of praying for a change that will probably never come, tired of hoping against hope that good can come out of undeniably bad circumstances. I hear myself trying to say hopeful things, and they sound hollow, especially in the midst of life's ugliest messes.

Maybe that's where the people of Nazareth were when Jesus circled back to His hometown in Mark 6. He had just come from Capernaum, where a long list of incredible miracles had occurred, the last of which had been the raising of Jairus' daughter from the dead (Mark 6:38-43). But although the stories of hope and healing must have traveled to Nazareth, the people stubbornly refused to believe that one of their own could have amounted to anything worth believing in (John 1:46). It's almost as if the whole town had a complex of hopelessness. Mark 6:5 tells us, "He could do no mighty work there," and verse 6 says, "He marvelled because of their unbelief."

This was actually the second time that Nazareth had rejected Jesus. The first time (Luke 4:16-30), they tried to kill Him for claiming to be the Messiah, and He miraculously escaped. Even then, Nazareth was an eye-witness to hope, but they were stubborn believers in hopelessness.

How horribly sad. How tragic. What miracles did He want to perform there? How many lives might have been changed? We'll never know. He would move on to feed the 5000 near Bethsaida, walk on the water, and would later spend much more time in Capernaum, where faith lived and miracles could abound. The people of Capernaum were no more deserving; they were just more believing.

It's been said that there is a storeroom in heaven filled with unclaimed blessings - gifts that a gracious heavenly Father longs to bestow, but that go unaccepted by His stubborn children.

Today, I choose to channel my stubbornness into an unflinching faith. I want all of the miracles, all of the blessings, and all of the goodness and mercy that God has for me and those I love (Psalm 23:6, 27:13, 100:5, Jeremiah 29:11-13). I'm dusting off the prayer requests that I've foolishly forgotten, and I'm taking them back to the throne with a renewed faith in the God Who is on that throne (Philippians 4:6, I Thessalonians 5:17, Hebrews 4:16).

Is there something that you've given up praying for? Pray for it again. Don't let the passage of time discourage you. God rarely works in our time, but His timing is always perfect. If you must be stubborn about anything, be stubborn about prayer (Romans 4:16-22, Hebrews 11:6, I Peter 1:7-8). Take all the energy you put into stressing, micro-managing, and griping, and expend that energy in prayer instead.

I refuse to be Nazareth, where faith was snuffed out and God's grace was stunningly rejected. I choose to believe in miracles, lost causes, the power of prayer, and the ever-working, unseen Hand of God. No matter how stubborn I may be on the surface, deep down I know that God has never let me down. So regardless of what my eyes have seen, I'll build up my hopes (Hebrews 11:1), and I'll make my home where faith lives.

YOUR PRESCRIPTION

Is your faith failing? Have you stopped asking God to move, because you don't believe He will? Ask God to give you a renewed faith in His sovereignty, His plan, and His unfailing love for you. Take your requests to Him, and believe that He is faithful.

SELF EXAMINATION
Is God speaking to you about a problem with your heart?

_____

_____

_____

_____

_____

TREATMENT PLAN
What steps do you need to take to address your heart problem?

_____

_____

_____

_____

_____

A Peg or Two

"Then I went down to the potter's house, and, behold, he wrought a work on the wheels. And the vessel that he made of clay was marred in the hand of the potter: so he made it again another vessel, as seemed good to the potter to make it." - Jeremiah 18:3-4

"My son, despise not the chastening of the Lord; neither be weary of his correction: For whom the Lord loveth he correcteth; even as a father the son in whom he delighteth." - Proverbs 3:11-12

"A new heart also will I give you, and a new spirit will I put within you: and I will take away the stony heart out of your flesh, and I will give you an heart of flesh." - Ezekiel 36:26

Scripture Reading: Daniel 4

I thought I was getting somewhere. I am forever trying to get my house and my life in order, and I peaked somewhere around mid-May. The house was cleaner than it had been in years. It could even be referred to as "company-ready" (a term I never would have dared to use earlier).

Then came summer - where the house is like a constantly revolving door, and toys, tools, and swimwear somehow transition seamlessly from the backyard to the kitchen table. And the little bit of control I thought I had has proven once again to be non-existent. For a brief time, I thought I had mastered the mess, but this season has taken me down a peg or two.

In Daniel 4, the mighty Nebuchadnezzar was definitely taken down a few pegs. As King of Babylon, Nebuchadnezzar was lord of all that he surveyed. He was a brutal warrior who had subdued many nations, and he thought of himself as a self-made man and a god in his own right. But the One True God would shatter that illusion, and would miraculously give this tyrant a testimony (I Timothy 1:15, II Peter 3:9).

Daniel 4 is actually narrated by Nebuchadnezzar himself. He proceeds to tell us that he had a dream. Only Daniel knows the meaning, because Daniel serves God, and the dream is from God. And the meaning is this: Nebuchadnezzar's success is not man-made; it is God-given. If Nebuchadnezzar can't get a hold of that truth, then God will get a hold of Nebuchadnezzar. He will be stripped of his power and dignity and will live in the wild like an animal. He will even take on the appearance of an animal, until he learns his lesson and glorifies God (I Chronicles 29:14, Psalm 24:1-2, 90:2, 97:9, Proverbs 21:1, Colossians 1:17).

While this may sound like a once-upon-a-time fairytale, history records that there was a period of seven years of unexplained inactivity in the reign of Nebuchadnezzar. Seven years of no conquests, no royal decrees, no major projects. I submit to you that God was working in those seven years, conquering Nebuchadnezzar's pride, decreeing his Sovereignty over the affairs of this kingdom and all others, and doing a major work in Nebuchadnezzar's heart (Daniel 5:18-21).

I also submit to you that God repeats this process over and over in each of our hearts - to win us, to keep us, and to grow us. In Jeremiah 18, the prophet is sent by God to go on a field trip to the local potter's house. His only purpose there is to watch and learn. He observes the absolute power that the potter has over the clay, to mold it, to break it, to use fire and water to refine and restore it. The irony: in this scenario (about 40 years before Nebuchadnezzar's dream in Daniel 4), the kingdom of Judah was the clay, and God was about to use Nebuchadnezzar to chasten His rebellious, but beloved people.

Many Christians bristle at the mention of "chastening". The very word conjures up images of an angry God doling out punishments like a judge in traffic court. But hidden within that scary word is a word that conjures up something else. That word is "chasing". In Daniel 4, God will break Nebuchadnezzar down, but He will also restore. In Jeremiah 18, the potter will break down the clay, but He will remold it into something better. God may be chastening you now - you may feel broken down, and all too aware of your own helplessness. But in the chastening, He is really chasing your heart - revealing His love, His power, and His plan in a million little ways, and molding you to be more like Him (Hebrews 12:5-6, I Peter 1:7).

The end result will be something far better. (Psalm 94:12, Isaiah 26:15-16, Ezekiel 36:26, Romans 5:3-5, 8:17-18, II Corinthians 4:17).

Don't be afraid to let God take you down a peg or two. Let the storms come, let the problems pile up, and let the God Who is chasing you get a hold of your heart and make it more like His.

YOUR PRESCRIPTION

Is God chasing your heart today? Stop running and start looking for the lesson He has for you. Whatever trial you're facing, God is in control of it, and He wants to do a work in your heart for His glory.

SELF EXAMINATION
Is God speaking to you about a problem with your heart?

_____

_____

_____

_____

_____

TREATMENT PLAN
What steps do you need to take to address your heart problem?

_____

_____

_____

_____

_____

Pick a Side

"And, behold, this day I am going the way of all the earth: and ye know in all your hearts and in all your souls, that not one thing hath failed of all the good things which the Lord your God spake concerning you; all are come to pass unto you, and not one thing hath failed thereof."
- Joshua 23:14

"And I have given you a land for which ye did not labour, and cities which ye built not, and ye dwell in them; of the vineyards and oliveyards which ye planted not do ye eat...And if it seem evil unto you to serve the Lord, choose you this day whom ye will serve...but as for me and my house, we will serve the Lord."
- Joshua 24:13, 15

"Therefore, my beloved brethren, be ye stedfast, unmoveable, always abounding in the work of the Lord, forasmuch as ye know that your labour is not in vain in the Lord." - I Corinthians 15:58

Scripture Reading: Joshua 24

I think I've gotten better. I pray I have, anyway. I'm a saint, but a saint is still a sinner - just a sinner saved by grace

(Ephesians 2:8-9). I have the Holy Spirit living in me, but to my shame, He doesn't always have the say that He should. I'm working on that (Romans 12:1-2).

It's not easy, because I operate in a fallen world in my failing flesh (way too much flesh, I might add). Every day is a battle, and so every day starts the same way - I get up, get in the Word, and pick a side.

Joshua knew about picking sides. In Joshua 24, Israel's leader is at the end of his life. His military career has been over for a while, and the twelve tribes have actually had a period of rest in the Promised Land (Joshua 23:1). But Joshua knows that soldiers get soft when there's nothing to fight for, and relative peace and prosperity have made Israel ripe for rebellion.

In his farewell address, Joshua delivers an ultimatum from the Lord. The covenant is before them, and it hasn't changed since Moses came down from Mount Sinai (Exodus 20). It's simple: no other gods, obey God's laws, serve Him with all your heart. To make obedience even easier, this covenant has abundant blessings attached, many of which the Children of Israel have already received. They have now moved into the "land flowing with milk and honey". They have traded their tents for turn-key homes that they didn't pay for and didn't build. They're living off a land that they didn't have to farm. The Canaanites (the previous residents) did all the sowing, and they are doing all the reaping.

The choice should be easy. God's resume is impeccable. He has kept every promise He's made to them. He's practically spoiled them with blessings, and He's soundly defeated all of their enemies. They may be warriors, but God has done all of their fighting for them. And yet, sin pulls at them. Idols abound in the houses that they've moved into, and remnants of pagan culture are already mingling with God's prescribed laws.

Through Joshua, God warns them to pick a side - His side, to be exact. Compromise is not an option. Assimilation is not an option. Joshua has made his choice, for himself and his family. No if's, and's, or but's, *we will serve the Lord* (Joshua 24:15).

The challenge still hangs in the air today. And to all the half-hearted, wishy-washy, excuse-making, "I have my liberty", fence-sitting Christians out there, I plead with you as an admittedly less-than-perfect friend who has danced around the fire and been burned (Galatians 5:13, 16-17, 24, I Corinthians 16:13). Pick a side.

Believe me, I get it. Sometimes, you just want to fit in. Sometimes, you just want to be one of the cool kids (John 12:42-43). Fighting is tiresome, lonely, and it's easier to just go with the flow (John 15:19, I John 2:15). Sin seems so effortless, so beguiling, and the world makes it look like so much fun.

Why am I making such a big deal of this? Because it's still a *big deal* to God. In Matthew 22:37-40, Jesus confirmed that the greatest commandment was to love the Lord your God with all your heart, soul, and mind. It's the way God loves us. That kind of love can't sit on a fence. It can't follow one day and flounder the next. It can't dance around the fire of sin and be faithful at the same time (Romans 8:6, II Corinthians 5:13-17, I Peter 2:11).

Most of all, when we love God that way, we can't be ungrateful, and we can't forget or ignore or cheapen the blessings that we have received (Psalm 18:35, 37:25-27, 63:3, Hebrews 2:3-4). We are compelled to be on the Lord's side and no other.

So where do you stand today? Would Joshua question your loyalty? Worse still, would Jesus question your love? If you have one foot on either side of the line, get on your knees, get your head in the Word, and let the Spirit move your heart to the Lord's side.

YOUR PRESCRIPTION

Are you all in? Are you talking to God and giving Him the chance to talk to you every day? Are you picking His side, and letting Him pick your passions, your plans, and your pursuits? Don't walk the line. Choose to serve Him with all your heart today.

SELF EXAMINATION
Is God speaking to you about a problem with your heart?

_____

_____

_____

_____

_____

TREATMENT PLAN
What steps do you need to take to address your heart problem?

_____

_____

_____

_____

_____

The Other Brother

"Then drew near unto him all the publicans and sinners for to hear him. And the Pharisees and scribes murmured, saying, This man receiveth sinners, and eateth with them." - Luke 15:1-2

"Then came Peter to him, and said, Lord, how oft shall my brother sin against me, and I forgive him? till seven times? Jesus saith unto him, I say not unto thee, Until seven times: but, Until seventy times seven." - Matthew 18:21-22

"Let all bitterness, and wrath, and anger, and clamour, and evil speaking, be put away from you, with all malice: And be ye kind one to another, tenderhearted, forgiving one another, even as God for Christ's sake hath forgiven you." - Ephesians 4:31-32

Scripture Reading: Luke 15:25-32

I've been struggling with a heart problem lately. Things have been bothering me - things that aren't my problem, my business, or my job to worry about. So let's cut right to the heart of the matter. I could make excuses all day (I have them in abundance), or I can get on my knees and confess my heart problem to the Great Physician.

In Luke 15, heart problems are abundant. The chapter starts with the real-life heart problems of the scribes and Pharisees, who are constantly taking note of the company that Jesus keeps (Verses 1-2). Frankly, they can't believe the audacity of Jesus. He claims to be the Son of God, and yet, He has no desire to rub shoulders with the temple's finest, the people who work so hard to prove their own worth before God and man (Luke 5:30-32).

As a matter of fact, He regularly snubs them (in their minds, anyway) in favor of the defiled, the unclean, and the people who have never gotten anything right or done anything good a day in their lives. He is turning their world upside down, giving the dregs of society the idea that they are loved by God, and the scribes and Pharisees hate Him for it (Matthew 5:20, 18:1-4, Luke 14:11, John 3:16-17, James 1:27).

Jesus responds with three parables that all picture the longsuffering love of God and His desire to redeem the lost (Romans 5:8, II Peter 3:9). The lost sheep (Luke 15:3-7), the lost coin (Verses 8-10), and the prodigal son are all clearly in need of finding and clearly treasured once they are found. But at the end of the prodigal son's story (Luke 15:11-32), we find the most distant and drifting of all the lost treasures - *the other brother*.

Like the Pharisees, the other brother has a debilitating heart problem. He measures worthiness by works, and all he knows is that he has been working all his life for his dad (Ephesians 2:8-9). His worthless younger brother, on the other hand, has shamed the family, squandered part of the estate, and I'm guessing was probably less than a contributor to the family's success before he ever even decided to up and leave.

The other brother is indignant. He's done everything right. He's the one worth celebrating, and he's the only one who should have any claim here.

If you're like me, you fight "Other Brother" tendencies all the time. We give up praying for and witnessing to people who seem too far gone. We write off our prodigal brothers and people in our everyday lives as hopelessly unworthy. We tire of waiting for them to come around, and we let insult, offense, and bitterness drive us away from the very people that God has called us to reach (Ephesians 2:10, I Peter 2:9).

And we can even play the "Other Brother" in the church. We know who needs to change, and it sure isn't us. We know what everyone else needs to be doing, and we're somehow oblivious to all of the foolish pride that is wrapped up in that mindset (Proverbs 11:2, 16:18). We think we've earned some position that gives us the right to rule others, when the truth is that we're incapable of earning anything in God's Kingdom. We forget how God's economy works, and we forget that our Savior and our Example walked this earth in humility - not honor (Philippians 2:3, 7-9).

Today, I am praying for an ever-growing spiritual self-awareness. I've figured this much out. I am wretched in my own right, plagued with heart problems, and I am the prodigal son and the other brother all rolled into one. But by God's grace, I long to be more like their Dad. I want to humble myself, run to others, and never stop welcoming them the way that God welcomed me.

YOUR PRESCRIPTION

Are you suffering from a heart problem today? Have you lost sight of how lost you were when God found you? Ask God to give you a greater spiritual self-awareness so you can humbly seek the lost and serve the saved for His glory.

SELF EXAMINATION
Is God speaking to you about a problem with your heart?

_____

_____

_____

_____

_____

TREATMENT PLAN
What steps do you need to take to address your heart problem?

_____

_____

_____

_____

_____

An Empty Life

"And when they came to Marah, they could not drink of the waters of Marah, for they were bitter: therefore the name of it was called Marah. And the people murmured against Moses, saying, What shall we drink? And he cried unto the Lord; and the Lord shewed him a tree, which when he had cast into the waters, the waters were made sweet." - Exodus 15:23-25a

"And she said unto them, Call me not Naomi, call me Mara: for the Almighty hath dealt very bitterly with me. I went out full and the Lord hath brought me home again empty."
- Ruth 1:20-21a

"O taste and see that the Lord is good: blessed is the man that trusteth in him." - Psalm 34:8

Scripture Reading: Ruth 1

The last year has taught me a lot. I'm learning that life doesn't have to be scheduled to the hilt to be full. I'm learning that emptiness can be a good thing, because it can make you available for opportunities you couldn't possibly anticipate. Most of all, I'm starting to understand that God requires room to work (II Chronicles 16:9, Isaiah 45:2, 54:2-3). He doesn't limit Himself to our petty little schedules, but rather, He does His greatest work when we have either voluntarily or involuntarily lost control of everything around us (Job 42:2, Psalm 135:6, II Peter 3:7-9).

In Ruth 1, Naomi had lost control of everything in her world. The years had been cruel. First, famine had struck Bethlehem, and in a desperate attempt to stop their world from spinning out of control, she and her husband, Elimelech, had moved their family to Moab. And that was when they really lost control. Elimelech died first, leaving Naomi with two boys to raise alone. After taking Moabite wives (probably not part of their parents' original plan), the sons die as well, leaving Naomi with a family full of helpless widows (Verses 3-5).

But the tide has turned in Bethlehem, and with nothing to her name, Naomi is drawn back to her hometown by the promise of bread (Ruth 1:6). She encourages her daughters-in-law to stay in Moab, knowing she has nothing to offer them, but of course, Ruth refuses to leave her side (Verses 15-18). And so this young widow follows her broken and bitter mother-in-law back to Bethlehem in search of a new life.

When Naomi finally arrives in Bethlehem, her old neighbors recognize her - but just barely. Those cruel years are etched on her face, and there's no more strapping husband, no little boys trailing behind her, just a young widow walking in her shadow, and an air of emptiness surrounding them both.

She tells them to call her "Mara", because God has dealt bitterly with her (Ruth 1:19-21). And in her bitterness, it escapes her that God was probably not involved in the decision to go to Moab, and probably not consulted when her sons took Moabite wives (committing them to stay in Moab until the sons' deaths ten years later). If Naomi's life was empty, it was because it was once full of decisions that emptied it of God.

There's another mention of the word Mara (or Marah) in the Old Testament. It shows up in Exodus 15:23-25. The Children of Israel had gone for 3 days without water in the wilderness. Desperate and complaining, they finally find water, but it is bitter and undrinkable. God shows Moses a tree and tells him to throw the tree into the water, and the water is immediately changed. I'm sure it's no coincidence that it reminds me of another tree that God used to change our bitter lives, when He sent His Son to die on Calvary's cross.

Like those bitter waters and our lost souls, Naomi's empty life immediately began to change the minute that she steered her course towards God (Isaiah 54:1-6). One of the greatest joys in reading the Book of Ruth is watching Naomi's emptiness turn into excitement. In a few short chapters, she goes from bitter to blessed. By Chapter 4, she's giddy as a schoolgirl, planning Ruth's wedding, and later playing grandma to Ruth's little boy (Verses 13-16). She may not have understood it right away, but her emptiness was actually a bittersweet gift, because it finally gave God room to work in her life in miraculous ways (Psalm 27:13, 30:5, Lamentations 3:15, 19-26, Romans 8:28).

Maybe you're feeling an emptiness today. Maybe it's not such a bad thing after all. Maybe it's just the opening that God needs to do a new thing (Isaiah 43:19). There is no empty life that He cannot fill to the fullest. There is no bitterness that He cannot turn into blessing. Give Him room to work, and He will do more than you can imagine.

YOUR PRESCRIPTION

Is God waiting to do a new thing in your life? Do you need to turn your heart in His direction? Do you need to turn it away from something that is turning you away from Him? Ask God to help you to make room for Him to work in your life.

SELF EXAMINATION
Is God speaking to you about a problem with your heart?

_____

_____

_____

_____

_____

TREATMENT PLAN
What steps do you need to take to address your heart problem?

_____

_____

_____

_____

_____

Backseat Driver

*"I will both lay me down in peace, and sleep:
for thou, Lord, only makest me dwell in safety."*
- Psalm 4:8

*"Thou wilt shew me the path of life: in thy pres-
ence is fulness of joy; at thy right hand there are
pleasures for evermore." - Psalm 16:1*

*"And I will bring the blind by a way that they
knew not; I will lead them in paths that they
have not known: I will make darkness light
before them, and crooked things straight. These
things will I do unto them, and not forsake
them." - Isaiah 42:16*

Scripture Reading: Matthew 8:19-32

When it comes to road trips, I think I'm a pretty good passenger. For all of the other control issues in my life, I actually manage to avoid being a backseat driver most of the time, mainly because I just enjoy being chauffeured around.

I wish I could say I avoid backseat driving in my spiritual life. I wish I could say that I just lean back and let God lead. But in my flesh, I want the wheel, and I want to know where we're going. I want to know when we're going to get there, and I want the power to "recalculate" when the road gets rough. I don't want any detours, delays, or unplanned stops. I want to map out the itinerary from beginning to end, cause I'm just crazy enough to think that I can.

In Matthew 8, Jesus has already had an extremely full day, to say the least. After preaching the Sermon on the Mount, He has been followed back down the mount by the multitudes. As He makes His way to the Sea of Galilee, he heals a leper, the centurion's servant, and then stops at Peter's house to heal Peter's mother-in-law, and those in need just keep coming.

It's now dark, and Jesus is still healing. The crowd follows Him right to the water (some will even get in boats to continue following). These people have no problem letting Jesus lead. They have seen His wisdom, His compassion, and His power on display all day long, and starting in Verse 19, Jesus reveals some truths about Himself that should put backseat drivers like myself to shame:

1. **The Cost of Discipleship** (Matthew 4:3-4, 6:25-34, Philippians 4:19) - In Verse 19, Jesus tells a would-be follower that the Son of Man has no place to lay His head. Although Jesus possessed untold riches in heaven, He walked this earth with virtually nothing to His name, and relied on His Father for each day's provision. Backseat drivers don't like surprises, and if you're like me, you want to know where everything is coming from - your next meal, your next paycheck, your next answer to prayer. But Jesus confirmed that the cost of discipleship is dependency, because dependency is the fertile ground that grows our faith.

2. **The Calm in the Storm** (Psalm 113:4-6, 135:6-7, Isaiah 26:3) - In Verses 23-27, Jesus is sleeping, while the disciples are panicking. A terrible storm has come

181

up - so terrible, that Matthew tells us the ship was covered with the waves. The storm doesn't wake Jesus; the disciples do. With one command, He stops the storm, and the disciples are stunned. He told them they had little faith, but more than 2000 years later, how much more reason do you and I have to stop questioning the power and sovereignty of God?

3. **The Conquering of Evil** (Luke 10:18, Romans 8:36-39, James 2:19, Revelation 20:1-10) - On the other side of the sea, Jesus is confronted by two demon-possessed men. After acknowledging Jesus as the Son of God (a truth even the disciples were just starting to wrap their heads around), the demons make another telling reference, "...art thou come hither to torment us before the time?" They're referring to the prophecy and the promise of Revelation 20, where death and hell are finally cast into the Lake of Fire. They knew that their time was short and God was sovereign. They knew Christ would conquer them one day, and we should know that we are "more than conquerors" in Him.

Today, I'm stretched out in the backseat of life. I'm wearing a t-shirt that says "Blessed", and I'm feeling it. In this very moment, the view is incredible, and I refuse to worry about the road ahead because I know the Driver has everything under control (Psalm 16:1, 32:8, Joshua 1:9, Isaiah 30:21, 42:16, Jeremiah 29:11). And though I'm not sure where we're headed next, I know that the final destination will make every last mile worthwhile.

YOUR PRESCRIPTION

Let God be God. Let your worries and fears take a backseat to His sovereignty. Ask Him to help you to trust Him to determine the course of your life - moment by moment, day by day, and so on. Remember Who He is. Remember how far He has brought you, and remember to enjoy the ride.

SELF EXAMINATION
Is God speaking to you about a problem with your heart?

_____

_____

_____

_____

_____

TREATMENT PLAN
What steps do you need to take to address your heart problem?

_____

_____

_____

_____

_____

The End Product

"He hath shewed thee, O man, what is good; and what doth the Lord require of thee, but to do justly, and to love mercy, and to walk humbly with thy God?" - Micah 6:8

"Pure religion and undefiled before God and the Father is this, To visit the fatherless and widows in their affliction, and to keep himself unspotted from the world." - James 1:27

"Even so faith, if it hath not works, is dead, being alone. Yea, a man may say, Thou hast faith, and I have works: shew me thy faith without thy works, and I will shew thee my faith by my works." - James 2:17-18

Scripture Reading: Matthew 23

I love lists. Frankly, they give me a sense of security, and for me, lists make life seem manageable. If I can put my list on a pretty piece of notepaper or in a cute little notebook, somehow that's even better. And once I start to actually check off a few of those items and see the end product of my work?

Well, then I really start to snuggle into the security of my own little world, represented by my own little list.

As I read Matthew 23, I get the impression that the Pharisees loved lists, too. They loved the security of believing that if they just accomplished A, B, and C, they were miles ahead of everyone else. But Jesus would plainly tell them (and us) that "doing right" should lead to "doing good", and hearts that truly love God will inevitably love others (James 2:14-16).

In Verses 1-7, Jesus outlines the practices of the Pharisees that focused on their checklists, their little worlds, and their control of the everyday people that they despised. Pharisees didn't care about caring for others. They didn't care about the physical needs or the spiritual needs of ordinary people. In their minds, ordinary people only existed to make them look *extraordinary*. And they preyed upon the well-meaning, everyday people who were searching for God, using the temple to make money off of those poor souls and shamelessly twisting the laws to profit off the penniless (Ezekiel 22:24-25).

In Verse 5, Jesus specifically spoke about phylacteries. These were little leather boxes that the Pharisees wore tied to their foreheads (still used by some today). Inside the box was tiny scrolls with scripture written on them. It made for a great show of holiness, but Jesus stressed and demonstrated humility as an indispensable ingredient of authentic holiness.

In Verse 13, Jesus even said that the Pharisees were keeping people away from heaven with their homemade brand of super-spirituality. They weren't leading people to God. They certainly weren't loving people to God, and for all of their glorified goodness, they weren't glorifying God.

Jesus continues His scathing rebuke in Verse 23, and this time, He tells them that tithing to the penny (another item on their checklist) is no substitute for giving from the heart and giving mercy to others (Psalm 82:3-4, Proverbs 3:27, Micah 6:8, II Corinthians 3:6, 8:1-5).

There's a great deal of cultural context built into this passage, but in Verses 27-29, Jesus boils it all down to this timeless truth: No matter how good you look on the outside, it's the inside that matters (Psalm 51:10, I Samuel 16:7, Proverbs 4:23, 21:2, Jeremiah 29:13). You can check all the lists you want, but if the only purpose has been to glorify and gratify yourself, you've missed the whole point of what God wants.

The Pharisees were all about self-help. They cared only about themselves. They wanted to make themselves look good. They helped themselves to whatever riches, privileges, and prestige they could. And the end product of all that self was only more self (Matthew 5:20, 12:35).

Our faith is not lived out in checklists of scriptural requirements; it is lived out in love (Matthew 5:8, I Corinthians 13, I Timothy 1:1,5, II Peter 1:3-9). Don't misunderstand me. Right living is important. Church attendance is important. Bible reading is important. Prayer is important. But these things are not just items on a spiritual checklist. These activities are meant to serve as heart-changers. They align our hearts to God, and the end product is a desire to glorify Him, to do for others, and to love others into alignment with Him as well.

As you're checking off your spiritual list today, think about what the end product will be. By all means, live *by* the Word of God, but live it *out* (and *give* it out) as well. Let it shine through you, let it touch others, and let it glorify no one but Him (Matthew 5:16). That's the end product that God desires.

YOUR PRESCRIPTION

Don't just check off the items on your spiritual to-do list. Ask God to align your heart to His, and glorify Him by loving others to Him.

SELF EXAMINATION
Is God speaking to you about a problem with your heart?

_____

_____

_____

_____

_____

TREATMENT PLAN
What steps do you need to take to address your heart problem?

_____

_____

_____

_____

_____

The Love & The Lag

"For the eyes of the Lord run to and fro throughout the whole earth, to shew himself strong in the behalf of them whose heart is perfect toward him." - II Chronicles 16:9a

"Then Jesus answering said unto them, Go your way, and tell John what things ye have seen and heard; how that the blind see, the lame walk, the lepers are cleansed, the deaf hear, the dead are raised, to the poor the gospel is preached. And blessed is he, whosoever shall not be offended in me." - Luke 7:22-23

"Let your conversation be without covetousness; and be content with such things as ye have: for he hath said, I will never leave thee, nor forsake thee. So that we may boldly say, The Lord is my helper, and I will not fear what man shall do unto me." - Hebrews 13:5-6

Scripture Reading: Luke 7:11-23

I don't know why I still struggle. Time and time again, I have seen the proof that God is in control, that His plan and His timing are perfect, and that He never has or will need my help.

And yet, my mind is forever working overtime, assuming what should happen next, growing impatient, and wondering why God isn't moving when I think He should.

In Luke 7, John the Baptist is in prison, and his mind is working overtime. His disciples come to him with stories of miracles - the blind, the lame, lepers, the deaf, and even the dead are benefitting from the ministry of Jesus. Miracles seem to be taking place everywhere, but not in John's prison cell. Left to the mercy of his enemies, this forerunner of the Messiah, the voice crying in the wilderness, the greatest prophet who ever lived (Luke 3:4-6, 7:26-28), and yes, the cousin of Jesus, has got to be wondering where *his* miracle is.

And so, in Verse 20, John sends an audacious, what-have-I-got-to-lose kind of question to Jesus, "Art thou he that should come? or look we for another?" His words seem to smack with impatience and assumption. Where are you, Jesus? Where's my miracle? What about me?

Verse 21 tells us that "in that same hour", Jesus performed another slew of miracles, and though none of them opened John's prison cell, I believe they were meant to open his eyes to the greater purpose of God.

In Verse 23, Jesus speaks directly to John and to anyone who doubts His perfect plan, "Blessed is he, whosoever shall not be offended in me."

It's as if He's telling John, "You can't take this personally. I know you want to get out of prison, but there are bigger things that need to be accomplished. It doesn't mean I don't love you, or I've forgotten about you. You just have to trust me."

We live with the mindset that "actions speak louder than words". And while that may be true in human interactions, it's a human standard that our stubborn and finite minds cannot accurately apply to a sovereign God (Psalm 119:160, Hebrews 11:6). We think we know how things should play out in a certain situation, and God seems to be lagging behind. But the only truth we know for certain is the character of our sovereign and loving God, and no matter what is or is not changing in your situation, that Character never changes (Exodus 3:14, Psalm 136, Hebrews 13:8, Revelation 1:8, 3:14, 19:11).

God is able to do anything, but He uses His power when and where He chooses, and we have to be okay with that. We can't take it personally. I can't tell you what the plan is, but I can unequivocally tell you *Who* He Is. Maybe that's why He refers to Himself as I AM - because the most valuable promise of all eternity is God's own unchanging character - the love that endures forever and the morning-by-morning faithfulness of our God (Lamentations 3:22-23, Malachi 3:6, Isaiah 43:25, 60:16).

Somewhere in your heart, you have to reconcile the love and the lag in your Father's actions. When God's plan seems to fall out of step, you might wonder on some level if He is still in control, still engaged in the things that concern you, still FOR you. Push those questions away. They are natural and they are normal, but if you entertain them for an extended period of time, they will rob you of blessings and blind you to His true working in your life.

No matter what miracles we do or do not receive, never forget that we live in the eternal miracle that Almighty God has chosen to love us as we are, to redeem us as we could not redeem ourselves, and to claim us as His own for eternity.

And at the end of the day, and even the end of life, that is all the miracle we truly need (John 11:25-26, 14:6, Revelation 1:8).

YOUR PRESCRIPTION

Have you found yourself wondering where God is? Have you questioned His love because you question His methods? Tell Him you trust Him, and ask Him for His perfect peace in your situation.

SELF EXAMINATION
Is God speaking to you about a problem with your heart?

_____

_____

_____

_____

_____

TREATMENT PLAN
What steps do you need to take to address your heart problem?

_____

_____

_____

_____

_____

My Ebenezer

"Then Samuel took a stone, and set it between Mizpeh and Shen, and called the name of it Ebenezer, saying, Hitherto hath the Lord helped us." - I Samuel 7:12

"He must increase, but I must decrease."
- John 3:30

"But God forbid that I should glory, save in the cross of our Lord Jesus Christ, by whom the world is crucified unto me, and I unto the world."- Galatians 6:14

Scripture Reading: I Samuel 7; Psalm 66

Today, it's personal. I have to admit, when I write about bits and pieces of my personal life, I cringe at the thought of someone reading them. But today, I have to admit something else - God has far exceeded my fragile and often faithless expectations.

The last year brought a world of change in our home. It started with the decision that I would leave my full-time job (at a point when it had just turned into my dream job in many ways), so that I could focus more on our boys and whatever ministry opportunities the Lord provided.

We really believed God had brought us to this point, but that belief didn't make it any less terrifying. We were effectively taking half of our income and throwing it out the window like it was unnecessary, while every fiber of my being told me that the money was absolutely necessary to our security.

Being the control freak that I am, I did everything I could to prepare for our great "leap of faith". I created spreadsheets on our expenses, stockpiled cash for emergencies, and drummed up about one-sixteenth of a mustard seed of faith. And the sad truth was this - my spreadsheets didn't add up, and my stock-pile wouldn't last through the winter.

And then there were the things that only God knew were coming - things that weren't even on my spreadsheets. A few minor but expensive illnesses, a few major but unanticipated car problems, and of course, the fallout from my general lack of accounting skills.

So now, I'm hear to provide the year-end report, if you will. Just like Samuel set up a stone as a remembrance of all that God had done for the Children of Israel (I Samuel 17), I want to raise my Ebenezer and tell you that God has done great things in my home, my heart, and in Heart Medicine (Psalm 66). I've spent more time at home, more time with my boys, more time in prayer, and more time in God's Word. I haven't published another book, or recorded another CD. I haven't gotten a new job, or a promotion or a raise. I've spent more time with kin-dergarteners than I have with corporate executives, and I haven't done much else.

But here's what matters - God has done much, and God alone has brought us through. He has met our needs and granted many desires. He has shown me just how blessed I am to have my husband, Paul, and He has brought us closer together than ever before. He has used us in ways we couldn't have imagined, and in spite of ourselves, He has grown our faith to at least an eighth of a mustard seed (Psalm 71:15-16, I Corinthians 1:28-29).

Imperfect as I am, I think I might have actually grown a little in the last year (Psalm 42:8, Matthew 16:25). And although I don't necessarily recommend unemployment as a growth strategy, I do recommend that you take a look at the things that you're counting on and clinging to in this life (Deuteronomy 30:19, Joshua 24:15, Psalm 20:7, Matthew 6:24-33). Are they the things that God would have you cling to? Or have they somehow taken His rightful place in your heart?

I recently read a devotional that challenged me to hone my hopes for the New Year down to one word - not a list of resolutions, but one single word. A word immediately came to mind, and I think 2016 gave me a head start on it. My word is "less". Less of me, and more of Him (John 3:30, II Corinthians 12:9). Less attention-seeking and more praise-giving. Less worrying, planning, trying and striving, in exchange for more trusting, relying, praying, and waiting. Less *stuff*, and more *substance*.

Maybe you faced struggles and unexpected challenges in the last year. Maybe your life has changed in ways that you weren't prepared for, and the things you thought you could count on have slowly ebbed away. Let the losses and the "less" of your life be an opportunity to experience *more* of God. Remember all that He has done for you, and resolve to know Him more in the coming year. He has brought you this far. Let His grace lead you home.

YOUR PRESCRIPTION

Raise your Ebenezer. Write down some of the blessings and burdens that you've had in the last year, and remember how God has been faithful. Commit the coming year to Him, and trust Him to work in ways beyond your imagination.

SELF EXAMINATION
Is God speaking to you about a problem with your heart?

_____

_____

_____

_____

_____

TREATMENT PLAN
What steps do you need to take to address your heart problem?

_____

_____

_____

_____

_____

The Morning Soundtrack

"Cause me to hear thy lovingkindness in the morning; for in thee do I trust: cause me to know the way wherein I should walk; for I lift up my soul unto thee." - Psalm 143:8

"I love them that love me; and those that seek me early shall find me." - Proverbs 8:17

"And ye shall seek me, and find me, when ye shall search for me with all your heart."
- Jeremiah 29:13

Scripture Reading: Psalm 63

I used to fill my head with a lot of garbage. When I was in my twenties and living alone in an apartment on Buffalo's West Side, every day started the same. Before I had even rubbed the sleep out of my eyes, the TV would be on, blaring with the vital "news" offered by a network morning show. It was the soundtrack of my morning. It seemed harmless enough. As a matter of fact, it seemed perfectly normal, and on some days even necessary.

Over my first cup of coffee, I would absorb the reports of violence and all the meaningless speculation, fear, worry and criticism, along with a side of celebrity gossip, the latest fashion trends, and an overall value system that is the opposite of everything in God's Word.

It made me feel informed. It made me feel relevant and current and cool. And it made me forget God.

By the time I headed out the door, there was hardly a thought of God in my head, and my days - and even more so, my nights - reflected it. I moved through them in a fog of self-sufficiency and self-centeredness, only acknowledging my need for God in moments of panic and problems.

Where am I going with all of this? I'm wondering - wondering how much pain I could have avoided, how much value I could have added, and how much joy I could have known during those years, if my morning soundtrack had been one that turned my heart towards God (Psalm 5:3, 55:17, 57:8, 92:2, 130:6, Lamentations 3:22-23, Isaiah 26:9).

In I Samuel 24, David is on the run. He and his ragtag followers are barely surviving in the wilderness of Engedi, and Saul is relentlessly pursuing them (I Samuel 23:13-14). Now, David is hiding with his men in the dark recesses of a cave, and King Saul has just walked in, totally unaware of their presence. Saul has ducked into the shadows of the cave to relieve himself. This king who is completely mad, completely violent and evil and out of control, and completely in the wrong, is *now* completely *vulnerable*, and David's men are urging him to seize the moment.

But despite the overwhelming temptation, David managed to restrain himself. He settles for cutting off a small piece of Saul's robe with his sword. With all of his men whispering in his ears and his own fear, anger, and indignation pounding in his head, somehow David heard the still, small voice of God, and I think it had a lot to do with his morning soundtrack.

Psalm 63 gives us a glimpse of that soundtrack. In the midst of his fugitive years, David talks about finding God early in the morning, longing for Him, depending on Him, and praising

Him. I love the resolve in Verse 8, *"My soul followeth hard after thee..."*, and again I have to wonder, am I that determined to incorporate God into every moment of every day - the early morning, the night watches, and everything in-between?

Throughout my life, any times of victory, peace, and contentment (even in trials) have been punctuated with the soundtrack of God's Word (Proverbs 16:3, 22:37, John 15:5, Romans 8:5, Philippians 4:8, I Thessalonians 5:16-18). And without exception, the ugliest and most regrettable moments of my life have played out against a soundtrack of the world's music and the world's mentality.

God is not distant. He is not hard to find or hard to hear, and He is certainly not irrelevant. We are the ones who fill our heads with garbage and clutter the soundtrack with things that are out of tune with God (Psalm 118:24, Isaiah 31:1, 55:6, Galatians 2:20, Ephesians 5:8, 19-20). The conversations that you choose to have and to hear. The music and media that you absorb. The thoughts you entertain and the company you keep. These are the things that determine how much of God's still, small voice gets through.

Play a soundtrack that points to God. Throughout each day, fill your head with things that fill your heart with Him, and long to hear Him say, "Well done."

YOUR PRESCRIPTION

Take an inventory of the things you're taking in. Fill your daily soundtrack with things that keep you in tune with God and get rid of the garbage. God will bless you for it.

SELF EXAMINATION

Is God speaking to you about a problem with your heart?

_____

_____

_____

_____

_____

TREATMENT PLAN

What steps do you need to take to address your heart problem?

_____

_____

_____

_____

_____

Swimming Upstream

"And if it seem evil unto you to serve the Lord, choose you this day whom ye will serve; whether the gods which your fathers served that were on the other side of the flood, or the gods of the Amorites, in whose land ye dwell: but as for me and my house, we will serve the Lord."
- Joshua 24:15

"And be not conformed to this world: but be ye transformed by the renewing of your mind, that ye may prove what is that good, and acceptable, and perfect, will of God." - Romans 12:2

"Love not the world, neither the things that are in the world. If any man love the world, the love of the Father is not in him. For all that is in the world, the lust of the flesh, and the lust of the eyes, and the pride of life, is not of the Father, but is of the world." - I John 2:15-16

Scripture Reading: James 1:18-27

I have some thoughts that keep playing over and over in my head, so much so that I'm writing this particular devotional in the wee hours of the morning.

That makes me think it's important.

Maybe I take my own insomnia too seriously, but I choose to believe that God is trying to tell me (and maybe you, by extension) something worth hearing.

I've been impressed lately with the concept of living a radical, intentional life - a life that defies cultural expectations and actively pursues God's expectations. It sounds like I'm stating the obvious, right? Of course, Christians are supposed to be different. And yet, looking at my own life, for all the changes I've tried to make by God's grace, I still find areas where I simply default to the cultural norm.

Culture is like a raging river. It's the current that flows through every aspect of our lives, and it's so easy to be swept downstream without even knowing it. To better illustrate my point, I want to introduce you to some of the Bible's greatest *upstream* swimmers:

1. **Job** - From the very first verse of the book that bears his name, Job is described as a standout in his culture - "a perfect and upright man" - and God Himself confirms the description in His conversation with Satan (Job 1:1, 8). There's no doubt he was the spiritual leader in his household, as evidenced by his regular sacrifices and prayers on behalf of his ten kids (Job 1:4-5). When his wife - and later his three friends - persecuted him in his darkest hours, Job resisted the temptation to blame God for his troubles and clung to the promise of his Redeemer (Job 2:8-10, 19:2-3, 25). Lastly, Job's trials ended when he "prayed for his friends" - an undeniably Christ-like response to *his* personal sufferings and *their* rush to judgment (Job 42:10, Matthew 5:43-45).

2. **Daniel** - As a teenager thrown into the decadence and depravity of the Babylonian culture, Daniel determined to intentionally live for God (Daniel 1:8). His upstream

swimming included everything from dietary choices to daily prayers, all at the risk of death. And in the king's court, where there was a constant contest for recognition and wealth among the "wise men", Daniel gave God the credit for his wisdom and sought no rewards from the king (Daniel 2:28, 5:17). God faithfully rewarded Daniel's faithfulness by giving Him the favor of no less than **four** pagan kings, dream-interpreting abilities, and a miraculous night in the lion's den (Daniel 6:3-5, 10, 20-22).

3. **Jesus** - It's no surprise that the Son of God defied cultural expectations, but it does us good to note some of the ways in which He did it. In a culture that valued property and wealth, Jesus had "no place to lay His head" (Matthew 8:20). In a society that valued piety and status, Jesus chose publicans and sinners over the Scribes and Pharisees (Mark 2:15-17). He regularly spoke of losing, dying, and giving - some of the least popular words in the vocabulary of His day (and our day, too). And He refused to help the Jews conquer Rome, choosing the greater battle of conquering sin and death through the cross and the empty tomb (Mark 8:35, Luke 6:38, Philippians 2:6-8, I Corinthians 15:54-55).

All day, every day, you are faced with choices - choices in your home, your activities, the way you spend your money, and the way you spend your time. It's easy to live life on auto-pilot, defaulting to culture, going with the flow, and floating downstream like everyone else (Romans 8:5-8, 13:14, II Timothy 2:3-4).

That's not how you run the race (I Corinthians 9:24, Hebrews 12:1-2).

The race requires determination, intention, and constant consultation with God and His Word. It requires being different and moving in a direction that is often the opposite of the obvious. In short, it requires an **upstream swim**.

Live your life intentionally. Look for those places where you've settled for the cultural norm instead of seeking God's better way. Let's pray about how we can live a life that truly honors God in every way, and then, let's go for a swim.

YOUR PRESCRIPTION

Keep flushing out those areas of your life where you need more of God's way and less of the world's way. Ask God to show you where He wants you to fight the current in our culture.

SELF EXAMINATION
Is God speaking to you about a problem with your heart?

_____

_____

_____

_____

_____

TREATMENT PLAN
What steps do you need to take to address your heart problem?

_____

_____

_____

_____

_____

Radical Departure

"Let your light so shine before men, that they may see your good works, and glorify your Father which is in heaven." - Matthew 5:16

"For ye were sometimes darkness, but now are ye light in the Lord: walk as children of light."
- Ephesians 5:8

"I am crucified with Christ: nevertheless I live; yet not I, but Christ liveth in me: and the life which I now live in the flesh I live by the faith of the Son of God, who loved me, and gave himself for me." - Galatians 2:20

Scripture Reading: Matthew 5:1-16

I had a rough start today - a lousy attitude here, a little impatience there, and a few poorly-chosen words to top it all off - not exactly an inspired beginning. I've done worse, but by God's grace, I could have done better.

How did God repay my foolishness? With a blessing.

Shortly after sending my boys off to school, I heard from a dear friend, who shared a story about a seed that we planted together more than a year ago (she planted wisely, and

I unwittingly helped) and the miraculous work that God had done with that seed. I was immediately convicted of the less-than-godly start to my day, and I was immediately reminded that God never fails to give me more than I deserve.

In Matthew 5, Jesus preaches what we refer to as the Sermon on the Mount. His public ministry is still in its early days. To date, He has been baptized by His cousin John, has survived the temptation in the wilderness by Satan, and has recruited his key disciples. Now, after healing countless people and gaining a following of "multitudes", He is talking about salt and light and bringing glory to God by the good works that we do (Verses 13-16). And the blueprint for those works is offered in the earlier verses of the chapter (Verses 3-11) known as the Beatitudes.

To law-abiding Jews, who still looked to the Old Testament writings of Moses as their personal blueprint, Jesus' words were downright radical. The Old Testament laws drew harsh and unforgiving lines between right and wrong. They decisively protected the innocent and punished the guilty. And in the hands of men, the Mosaic laws had served as the foundation for an "every man for himself" society, where personal rights ruled and the heart of God had little place (sound familiar?). People were throwaways - cast out, spit upon, and stoned for violations of the law. There was little opportunity for redemption, mercy was a rare commodity, and compassion was hard to come by.

And while God is holy and cannot tolerate sin, their man-made version of the law did not represent His heart (Romans 5:1-10, Galatians 3:23-25, 4:4-6). The very heartbeat of God is revealed in the Beatitudes. Responding to cruelty with kindness, seeking and pursuing peace, giving mercy when it's least deserved - these are the behaviors of God Himself (Micah 6:8, John 3:16-17, Ephesians 2:8-9).

Though there had to be a payment for sin, He chose to send His Son to pay it for us - the ultimate act of meekness, mercy, and reconciliation, but by no means the last act of that kind by God. How many times have you failed Him? And yet He has blessed you. How many times have you denied Him? And yet your salvation is sealed by the blood of His own Son. How many times have you ignored Him? And yet, He hears you when you humbly call on Him.

Jesus' behavior was radical - sin was sin, repentance was required, but mercy was always within reach. It was a departure from the unforgiveness of the day, and a light that revealed a side of God that so many had missed (John 3:19, 12:35, 36).

And just as Jesus stood out against the backdrop of the law-wielding Scribes and Pharisees of His day, we need to stand out as a mercy-giving light in the rights-driven culture of our day (Matthew 5:43-45, Luke 6:35, Ephesians 5:8, I Peter 3:8-12).

We need to resist the temptation to beat people over the head with right and rights, and choose to love when it's least deserved. That kind of love opens a heart to God's conviction - not man's condemnation - and brings about the radical change of a sinner saved by grace.

Love radically, give radically, and FORgive radically. Respond to people in a way that defies their every-man-for-himself expectations. Be a radical departure from the way of the world and a bright light that leads the way out of darkness. **Be** the attitude of Christ.

YOUR PRESCRIPTION

Is there a situation where your light isn't shining so well? Ask God to give you a radical, Christ-like response to a dark situation. Be a light where light is least expected.

SELF EXAMINATION
Is God speaking to you about a problem with your heart?

_____

_____

_____

_____

_____

TREATMENT PLAN
What steps do you need to take to address your heart problem?

_____

_____

_____

_____

_____

The Carriers

"He that goeth forth and weepeth, bearing precious seed, shall doubtless come again with rejoicing, bringing his sheaves with him."
- Psalm 126:6

"And even to your old age I am he; and even to hoar hairs will I carry you: I have made, and I will bear; even I will carry, and will deliver you." - Isaiah 46:4

"And they come unto him, bringing one sick of the palsy, which was borne of four. And when they could not come nigh unto him for the press, they uncovered the roof where he was: and when they had broken it up, they let down the bed wherein the sick of the palsy lay. When Jesus saw their faith, he said unto the sick of the palsy, Son, thy sins be forgiven thee." - Mark 2:3-5

Scripture Reading: Mark 2:1-12

I used to carry a lot of guilt, because I was more blessed than most. While many people had bad parents, a bad environment, and bad influences, I pretty much had the deluxe life package - good parents, a home in the burbs, a pastor for a dad, Christian school, and it goes on and on. So when I messed up, it seemed way worse than other people's messes. I had no excuses, no scapegoat - just my own stupid decisions and a rebellious heart.

When I finally came to my senses, redemption seemed out of reach. How could God forgive so much wrong from someone He had treated so right? Blinded and bound by my own shame, I just couldn't find my way back.

That's where the carriers came in.

In His mercy, God put people in my path - people who helped me to see myself as forgiven, people who carried me back to the cross.

In Mark 2, we meet a quartet of carriers. They aren't just moved with compassion for their friend. Their compassion *causes* them to move.

Jesus is in a house in Capernaum, and the town is in a frenzy. In the previous chapter (Mark 1) Jesus cast out demons, healed Peter's mother-in-law, and cured a leper, telling him to keep the miracle to himself. The leper did the exact opposite (Mark 1:44-45), and now, Jesus can't go anywhere without drawing a crowd. So He is literally preaching to a packed house (Mark 2:1-2), standing room only, with an audience overflowing into the street.

This is where the carriers come in - four guys, rallying around their desperately sick friend. They carry him on his bed to the house, but they can't penetrate the wall of people. Many would have given up at this point, but these guys refuse to be deterred.

Instead of turning around and going home, they press on and carry their friend up to the roof of the house. They then proceed to dismantle the roof and lower their friend, sickbed and all, to the feet of Jesus. Needless to say, Jesus is pleased - even somewhat impressed. Verse 5 tells us that their faith caught His attention, and He healed their friend, both spiritually and physically.

There's a lot to be said for being a carrier. **God the Father is a carrier and a restorer** (Psalm 10:14, 23:3, 34:18, 68:5, 91:12, Lamentations 3:22, 32, Micah 7:18-19). Throughout the Old Testament, He pleads with His chosen people to let Him carry them - no matter how far they stray. He is constantly begging them to stop relying on idols, their own wisdom and their own work, so that He can forgive, restore, and bless them.

Christ was a carrier (Isaiah 53:11, 61:1-3, Romans 8:34, 15:1-3, Hebrews 7:25, 9:28, 13:13). He bore our sins on the cross, and He continues to plead with His Father on our behalf. He came to this earth to carry us to His Father, knowing we could never make the journey on our own.

And we are called to be carriers (Isaiah 58:6-12, I Corinthians 13:7-8a, Galatians 6:1-3, I Peter 4:10). And therein lies the challenge. I'm not even going to ask if you know someone who needs carrying, because I know you do. All around you are people who need to be carried - carried to the cross (Jude 21-23), carried to the throne of grace (Hebrews 4:16), and even just carried through the day (Psalm 3:2, 6:6, Matthew 11:28).

The question is - do we persist and pursue? Do we turn around and go home when we hit a wall, or does our compassion move us so much that we carry as far and as long as it takes to get them to Jesus?

I thank God someone carried me - I know I didn't make it easy. And I want to keep carrying others as far as I can, for as long as God lets me.

My plea to you - carry the lost, carry the hurt, and the helpless, and the broken, and never stop *caring*. And until you finally get to the feet of Jesus, *carry on*.

YOUR PRESCRIPTION

Let your compassion move you. Carry someone to God in prayer, but also make a tangible effort to carry them wherever and however they need to be carried - for God's glory. Christ carried you. Now it's time to carry someone to Him.

SELF EXAMINATION
Is God speaking to you about a problem with your heart?

_____

_____

_____

_____

_____

TREATMENT PLAN
What steps do you need to take to address your heart problem?

_____

_____

_____

_____

_____

Morning People

"Behold, the eye of the Lord is upon them that fear him, upon them that hope in his mercy."
- Psalm 33:18

"It is of the Lord's mercies that we are not consumed, because his compassions fail not. They are new every morning: great is thy faithfulness. The Lord is my portion, saith my soul; therefore will I hope in him. The Lord is good unto them that wait for him, to the soul that seeketh him."
- Lamentations 3:22-25

"For, behold, I am for you, and I will turn unto you...Then the heathen that are left round about you shall know that I the Lord build the ruined places, and plant that that was desolate: I the Lord have spoken it, and I will do it."
- Ezekiel 36:9a, 36

Scripture Reading: Ezekiel 37:1-14

I've always been a morning person, probably because I've always had to be. I'm in a short-lived but wonderful season right now, where I don't necessarily have to be up and out of the house first thing every morning. And yet, I am still usually up before 5 a.m., charging into the day as if the clock is chasing me.

The problem with charging into the day is that it's easy to charge right past the things that matter most. The Bible tells us in Lamentations (3:19-26) that the Lord's mercies are new every morning. Boy, is that ever a promise to hang your hat on. I have yet to live through a day where I didn't need my daily dose of God's mercies. Oh, don't get me wrong, I have skipped my spiritual breakfast more than once, but never without regretting it somewhere along the way.

In Ezekiel 37, the prophet has a vivid vision for his people. As a priest and a Jewish exile in Babylon (Ezekiel 1:1-3), Ezekiel knew the pains of spiritual starvation. He and the other exiles were far from their beloved Jerusalem, far from their temple, their homes, and their heritage. And they had seen what exile had done to their northern counterparts. When Assyria had defeated the Northern Tribes of Israel some 150 years earlier, exiling many of those people, they had all but lost their identity (II Kings 17:5-6, Ezekiel 23:33). Their religion (or what was left of it), their bloodlines, their borders - everything had been polluted beyond recognition.

Now, that same hopelessness was settling over the exiles from the Kingdom of Judah. But in Chapter 37, God paints a picture of promise, and in the midst of spiritual starvation, God serves up a helping of morning mercies.

He shows Ezekiel a valley of dry bones, and the opening outlook is bleak (Verses 1-2). It's clear that these bones haven't seen life in a long time, and they are as dried up as an exile's hope of home. But these dry bones are no match for the restorative powers of God. As Ezekiel watches, the bones begin to rattle, and then they begin to build, reassembling themselves before his eyes.

Next, flesh and muscle and skin weave themselves on top of the bones (Verses 7-8). But here's the key. The bones are now bodies, but they require one last miracle, one more mercy before they can claim to be alive - *they need the breath of God.* God commands the four winds to breathe *His* life into these bones, and His breath not only resuscitates life, it resuscitates hope (Verses 9-10). The exiles will have a future. They will have a home, and a heritage, and hope - regardless of their defeats - because they have a God Who will save them (Psalm 18:3, 31:16, 66:16-20, Isaiah 40:1-2, Zephaniah 3:17).

Many of us are willing to let God build our lives, but how many of us actually let Him *breathe* into our life every day? We wake up each morning and take for granted the gifts of God - our homes, our families, our faith, our country - and we fail to get down on our knees and claim the mercies that we so desperately need to preserve those things. We fail to ask God to breathe HIS life into them, and we charge into the day destined to live a dry and tenuous life, starved of morning mercies.

When it comes to God's mercies, we all need to be morning people, and an encounter with God should be as much a part of our morning routine as toothbrushing (Psalm 5:3, 55:17, 92:2, 143:8, Isaiah 33:2, 50:4, Mark 1:35). Communion with God is hydration for the soul, and whether you get a sip or a saturation of His presence, it will bless your day and breathe life into your every move.

Get your morning mercies every day. Charge into your day hand-in-hand with God, knowing that He is for you (Deuteronomy 3:22, I Samuel 17:47, Romans 8:31, 37). Ask Him to breathe Himself into every aspect of your life. You may feel like you are in a dry season, but I'm here to tell you - rain is in the air, mercies are on the horizon, and by God's grace, hope is alive.

YOUR PRESCRIPTION

Don't skip breakfast. Even if it's just for a matter of minutes, meet with God every morning. He can breathe life into everything you hope for, and even what you thought was dead.

SELF EXAMINATION

Is God speaking to you about a problem with your heart?

_____

_____

_____

_____

_____

TREATMENT PLAN

What steps do you need to take to address your heart problem?

_____

_____

_____

_____

Me & My Big Mouth

"Except the Lord build the house, they labour in vain that build it: except the Lord keep the city, the watchman waketh but in vain. It is vain for you to rise up early, to sit up late, to eat the bread of sorrows: for so he giveth his beloved sleep." - Psalm 127:1-2

"Every wise woman buildeth her house: but the foolish plucketh it down with her hands."
- Proverbs 14:1

"For thus saith the Lord God, the Holy One of Israel; In returning and rest shall ye be saved; in quietness and in confidence shall be your strength: and ye would not. But ye said, No; for we will flee upon horses; therefore shall ye flee: and, We will ride upon the swift; therefore shall they that pursue you be swift." - Isaiah 30:15-16

Scripture Reading: Jeremiah 44

I remember my dad talking more than once about having an "economy of words". His point was this - use your words sparingly and spend your words wisely, and they will have a greater impact. And although I know he was right, I often catch myself in a spending *spree* of words, spouting half-baked advice, unsolicited opinions, and counter-productive commentary. My big mouth gets me into trouble on a regular basis.

In Jeremiah 44, big mouths abound. The setting is Egypt. Jewish refugees, the remnant of Judah - following the siege and subsequent burning of Jerusalem by the Babylonians - are in full, unflinching rebellion against God (Verses 1-2).

First, God said to get rid of the idols. In truth, He had been saying it for hundreds of years. *They never listened.* While they were still participating in immoral pagan worship rites and baby sacrifices, God sent prophets (Jeremiah included) to tell them over and over that judgment (in the form of Babylon) was coming (Verse 4). *They never listened.* After countless of their own had been slaughtered or carried away and Babylon wreaked its final destruction on Jerusalem, God told the survivors not to go to Egypt (Verses 6-12, Isaiah 30). He begged them to return to Him. *They never listened.*

Now, the Lord sends Jeremiah for one last showdown with the transplanted remnant.

Generations worth of rebellion have finally come full-circle. They have left the Promised Land, devastated and cursed by their own sin, and have willfully returned to Egypt, the original land of their slavery. And God's Word is clear. Their escape plan has taken them completely off the course of God's plan, and with the exception of a few witnesses to tell the sad tale, this remnant will never see Jerusalem again (Verses 11-14).

A startling truth (startling to me, anyway) comes to light in the middle of the chapter - a bunch of big-mouthed, know-it-all women were at the core of the rebellion (Verses 15-19). Now I have no intention of degrading my own gender, but I can't deny that I felt a little tug of conviction as I read this passage about women who thought they had all the answers.

Their rationalization for rebellion is even more startling. They lift themselves up as the ones who brought protection and prosperity to their homes. They insist that life was good when they worshipped idols, and it was because of the idols that *they* chose. They give their idols the credit for every blessing and give God the blame for every evil.

Speaking over their own husbands, these women brazenly tell the man of God, *"...we will not hearken unto thee. But we will certainly do whatsoever thing goeth forth out of our own mouth..."* (Verses 16-17). Those words make me want to duck and cover. Who among us is *stupid* enough to think that we're *smart* enough to run our homes without God?

And yet, if I'm honest, I can think of times where I had a plan laid out well before I laid down my prayer. Too often, I hear myself brazenly telling God what He needs to do next, expecting Him to endorse *my* wisdom, rather than seeking *His* (Psalm 37:4-6, 46:10, Proverbs 3:5-6, Matthew 6:33, John 10:27, 15:5, Philippians 4:6-7).

I believe that, by God's grace, I am good for my family. I love them with all my heart. I keep them from living on pizza, wearing the same clothes for weeks on end, and turning the house into a barn. And sometimes, I think they actually appreciate it - even if only for a second. But I'm not kidding myself that I'm the one doing the protecting and the providing and the saving here. *My home needs God.* YOUR home needs God. And if we're not careful, in our fierce determination to protect our homes by our own means and in our own wisdom, we can unwittingly destroy them (Proverbs 14:1, 31:25-31, Luke 6:48, Colossians 3:18, Titus 2:3-5).

Me and my big mouth have caused trouble more than once, but me and my God have come through more troubles than I can count. And the truth is, *God* took care of the trouble, and I often *was* the trouble. God brought the blessing, and I was just blessed. And for all my so-called wisdom, the best wisdom is this: my home works best, when God is in charge.

YOUR PRESCRIPTION

Who's running your home? Is God guiding every major deci-sion, or have you somehow decided that YOU know what's best? Ask God to be the center of your heart and your home and the central authority in everything.

SELF EXAMINATION
Is God speaking to you about a problem with your heart?

_____

_____

_____

_____

_____

TREATMENT PLAN
What steps do you need to take to address your heart problem?

_____

_____

_____

_____

_____

Storm System

"Hear me speedily, O Lord: my spirit faileth: hide not thy face from me, lest I be like unto them that go down into the pit." - Psalm 143:7

"The Lord is nigh unto all them that call upon him, to all that call upon him in truth. He will fulfil the desire of them that fear him: he also will hear their cry, and will save them."
- Psalm 145:18-19

"On the left hand, where he doth work, but I cannot behold him: he hideth himself on the right hand, that I cannot see him: But he knoweth the way that I take: when he hath tried me, I shall come forth as gold." - Job 23:9-10

Scripture Reading: Psalm 143

This imperfect woman has been tested and retested lately. And although the house is still standing and the kids are still alive, I feel like my imperfections are oozing out all over the place. Storms (even late winter snow storms) have a way of bringing your inner storms to the surface. Throw in a week when your husband is away, a minor car accident, and a few small household disasters, and you've got an entire storm system. Despite my best attempts at holding it all together, recent days have exposed nerve endings I didn't even know I had.

In Psalm 143, I think David could relate. He talks about an overwhelmed spirit and a desolate heart (Verse 4), and he begs God to hear him without judging him - all the hallmarks of a man whose inner storm system has just bubbled to the surface.

Some Bible scholars believe this Psalm was written while David was on the run from King Saul (I Samuel 23). Others say he wrote it while running from his own treacherous son, Absalom (II Samuel 16). Either way, David knew desperation. And although he was being pounded by a relentless external storm, his prayer seems to focus more on the storms that raged in his own heart. In 3 of the verses (Verses 3, 9 and 12) David asks the Lord to save him from his enemies. We all have those moments, don't we? This fallen world is against us every day - in the forms of sickness, danger, loss, and need. The world wars against our families, our homes, and our churches. There are storms out there, and often, they threaten a bigger fallout than record snowfalls.

But although he is acutely aware of the external threats, in twice as many verses (Verses 4, 6, 7, 8, 10 and 11) David asks God to save him from *himself*. Boy, can I relate to that. Sometimes it's not so much what the storms *do* to me as it is what they bring *out* of me. And maybe that's got something to do with God's purpose in the problem. My natural response to storms betrays just how much hold my sin nature still has on me.

David openly outlines his heart condition, but he also shares the prescription that made him a man after God's own heart (I Samuel 13:14, Acts 13:22). Starting in Verse 5, David implements a very deliberate, intentional, and prepared response to this storm. He remembers the works of God. He thinks about Who God is and what He has done. He stretches His hands to God, and asks God for a speedy deliverance (Verses 6-7, Psalm 63:1, 8, Isaiah 26:9) - and I don't think there's anything wrong with that. Don't be afraid to tell God that you've reached the end of your rope, because that's where your much-needed dependency on Him begins (John 15:4-5, II Corinthians 12:9).

David then asks God to cause Him to *hear*, to cause Him to *know*, and to *teach* Him (Verses 8-10). That takes the senselessness out of a storm. If it only ravages the outside, then a storm is *sadly* senseless, but if it changes us for the better on the inside, then maybe by God's grace, we really can gain from the pain (Psalm 119:71, 124, James 1:3, I Peter 1:7).

I don't like this process any more than you do, but I've come to appreciate its necessity. After all, if we really want to do the kind of deep cleaning in our hearts that we say we do, nothing washes all the garbage up onto the beach like a good storm (Psalm 51:7-10, 139:23-24). And I'm sorry to say that, on more than one occasion, God has gently whispered to my heart about something that needed to change, but it wasn't until I gasped at my own knee-jerk response to some life storm that I took Him seriously.

Honestly, I don't know what your storm is today. Chances are, it would make my little mini storms seem inconsequential. But my God is not inconsequential. He conjures storms, and He quiets them. He hears prayers, and He answers them. And He uses storms to shape a stony heart and a rock-hard head like mine, and I praise Him for it.

YOUR PRESCRIPTION

Take a shower in the storm. Let God use your storm to reveal any part of your heart that needs to be washed clean. He will make a way, but if you ask, He will also make a change in you.

SELF EXAMINATION
Is God speaking to you about a problem with your heart?

_____

_____

_____

_____

_____

TREATMENT PLAN
What steps do you need to take to address your heart problem?

_____

_____

_____

_____

_____

The Pursuit of God

"For thou, Lord, art good, and ready to forgive; and plenteous in mercy unto all them that call upon thee." - Psalm 86:5

"Then Agrippa said unto Paul, Almost thou persuadest me to be a Christian. And Paul said, I would to God, that not only thou, but also all that hear me this day, were both almost, and altogether such as I am, except these bonds."
- Acts 26:28-29

"This is a faithful saying, and worthy of all acceptation, that Christ Jesus came into the world to save sinners; of whom I am chief." - I Timothy 1:15

Scripture Reading: Acts 26

There are days that I'm just not feeling it. I want to tell you that I roll out of bed every morning with a hymn in my heart, looking forward to my morning meeting with God. But although God and I do have a morning routine, His heart is almost always in it more than mine. Take this morning - I have my devotionals in front of me, scripture readings, and prayer requests on my heart, and moments later, I'm watching a cute video on Facebook about a little girl who won't give her mom five minutes alone in the bathroom.

How does that happen? How does my pursuit of God fall flat so quickly? Social media is an easy scapegoat, but my spiritual ADD (Attention Deficit Disorder) has even lured me away from my Bible to instead do loads of laundry - and I don't even *like* laundry. It all boils down to this: I am forever dependent on God's relentless pursuit of me.

In Acts 26, we see God in pursuit. After 2 years in prison, Paul is brought before Agrippa to plead his case as a preacher of the gospel. Let me give you some background on Agrippa. He is the 4th generation of the powerful Herodian dynasty. His maternal grandfather and paternal great-grandfather (yes, his family was that messed up) was Herod the Great (Matthew 2), the Herod who tried to use the wise men to find the Christ child and eventually murdered all the baby boys in Bethlehem.

It was Agrippa's mother, Herodias, who received John the Baptist's head on a platter from her then-husband and brother-in-law (I told you they were messed up) and Agrippa's uncle, Herod Antipas (Mark 6:14-28). Agrippa's Uncle Antipas was also the Herod who conducted one of the mock trials of Jesus before sending him back to Pilate for judgment (Luke 23:6-12).

And Agrippa's father, Agrippa I, was the Herod in Acts 12, who killed the apostle James (the brother of John), persecuted the church, and died an ugly, wormy death for lifting himself up as a god.

Now Agrippa is king, under the auspices of Rome, and he has been asked by the Roman governor, Festus, to try Paul. Beside him sits his wife, Bernice, who also happens to be his sister (more of the same mess). Agrippa is a man born in sin and steeped in sin his whole life. He is the last generation of a family that has shaken its fist in the face of God for years. And yet, just like you and me, Agrippa is the object of the pursuit of God.

God sends Paul, the chief of sinners (I Timothy 1:15), to share his testimony with Agrippa, and Paul holds nothing back. After profiling his early life as a student of Jewish law, Paul explains how he shook his own fist in the face of God as a hunter and persecutor of Christians (Acts 8, 26:9-11). He then tells Agrippa of his conversion on the road to Damascus and the moment when God's pursuit finally caught up with him (Acts 9, 26:13-18).

Agrippa's response may well be one of the saddest quotes in the whole Bible, "**Almost** thou persuadest me to be a Christian." Paul replies with a final prayer on behalf of Agrippa, Bernice, and their court (Acts 26:28-29). He is voicing the heart of God, who is not willing that ANY should perish - not even a Herod (Daniel 9:9, Romans 5:6-8, II Peter 3:9).

Wherever you are today, know that you are the object of God's pursuit. There are no coincidences in the Christians that He has put in your path, the pull at your heart, or even the fact that you are reading this devotional. And if you are pursuing the heart of someone else in prayer, never doubt that you are voicing the heart of God, and He is right beside you in the pursuit of that lost soul (Psalm 17:7-8, John 3:16-17, I John 3:1, Jude 1:23).

Today, I'm letting the laundry go. Like Paul, I was a high-ranking sinner that Jesus chased down a dark road. But now, I am blessed beyond measure, and I am gladly, gratefully, and gloriously giving in to the pursuit of God.

YOUR PRESCRIPTION

Stop running. Give in to the God that gave all for you. And never stop pursuing others on His behalf. Pray for the lost, believing that no sinner is too sinful to be saved.

SELF EXAMINATION
Is God speaking to you about a problem with your heart?

_____

_____

_____

_____

_____

TREATMENT PLAN
What steps do you need to take to address your heart problem?

_____

_____

_____

_____

_____

The Gift & The Giver

"Give therefore thy servant an understanding heart to judge thy people, that I may discern between good and bad: for who is able to judge this thy so great a people? And the speech pleased the Lord, that Solomon had asked this thing." - I Kings 3:9-10

"Every good gift and every perfect gift is from above, and cometh down from the Father of lights, with whom is no variableness, neither shadow of turning." - James 1:17

"For God, who commanded the light to shine out of darkness, hath shined in our hearts, to give the light of the knowledge of the glory of God in the face of Jesus Christ. But we have this treasure in earthen vessels, that the excellency of the power may be of God, and not of us."
- I Corinthians 4:6-7

Scripture Reading: I Kings 3

God is really good to me. In fact, I got a little godly spoiling recently through a dear friend of mine. We are both girly girls who share a love for makeup. My friend recently planned to purchase some cosmetic items at the mall, and she knew that her purchase came with a free gift. Upon her invitation, we went to the mall together, and even though I made no purchases of my own, my friend graciously bestowed her free gift on me.

I was like a kid at Christmas. Within minutes of getting home, I was sorting through my new supply of girly gifts and dolling myself up just for the fun of it. But as much as I love the stuff, that love doesn't compare to my affection for the *giver*, who went out of her way to show me a special kindness and shared a part of herself with me.

In I Kings 3, God shares a part of Himself with Solomon. Appearing to the fledgling king in a dream, God asks, "What shall I give thee?" Could there be a better offer? The God of the Universe opens His storehouses and says, "What do you want, Solomon? Just name it, and it's yours."

Solomon is loved by the Lord, and He loves the Lord in return (II Samuel 12:24, I Kings 3:3, I John 4:19), but he's already made a few mistakes. Most notoriously, he has aligned himself with Egypt by marrying Pharaoh's daughter (I Kings 3:1). Knowing Solomon's heart, and also knowing his weaknesses, it seems God is trying to get his attention before he veers too far off course. And at first, Solomon's affection for the Giver outweighs his desire for the gifts, and God rewards His request for wisdom with promises for riches and honor as well.

But as with all of His gifts, God requires one thing from Solomon - *singular devotion* (I Kings 3:14). It's not a new commandment. In fact, it's a reiteration of the first commandment (Exodus 20:3, Deuteronomy 6:5, Matthew 22:37-38). Solomon knows that obedience and God's blessing go hand in hand, and yet, his God-given wisdom will tarnish with time, and his end will tell that even the greatest gifts lose their luster, when they are detached from the Giver.

By I Kings 11, Solomon is a king drowning in his own excess. You know the numbers - 700 wives, 300 concubines, and a heart turned from God (Verse 3). And in righteous judgment, the Giver is forced to tear the kingdom away from Solomon (Verses 11-13).

How can a gift of godly wisdom implode like that? It all goes back to the Giver. Our lives are full of gifts from God, but the true value of those gifts depends on our devotion to Him. Without that devotion, the full potential of His gifts is never achieved. And when the gift becomes more important to us than the Giver, when His glory no longer shines through it, that gift becomes just another knick knack, just another parlor trick, just another drop in the bucket of our own excess.

God has given me many good things, but in the last few years, I have become keenly aware that they don't work without Him. I believe He has given me a marriage, a home, a family, and a purpose so that I can work those things out with Him (II Corinthians 9:8, Ephesians 3:20, Philippians 2:12-13) - not so I can simply take them and run. He wants to use my life (and yours) to point people to Him. He has filled my life with potential that I could never achieve on my own, so that I can continue to grow in Him, to learn dependence on Him, and to draw others to His grace (II Corinthians 4:7, 12:31-13:1, Ephesians 2:10).

Whatever you do, *never detach the gifts from the Giver.* Let those blessings cement His place in your heart - not *take* His place. He is the light in their luster. He is the source of their shine. And the Gift behind every gift is the Giver Himself (Genesis 15:1, II Corinthians 9:15, Hebrews 11:6).

YOUR PRESCRIPTION

Have you taken the Giver for granted? Have you let His gifts take His place in your heart? If so, give those gifts and your affections back to Him, and ask Him to bring about the purpose and potential that He originally intended.

SELF EXAMINATION
Is God speaking to you about a problem with your heart?

_____

_____

_____

_____

_____

TREATMENT PLAN
What steps do you need to take to address your heart problem?

_____

_____

_____

_____

In the Knowing

"For he taught his disciples, and said unto them, The Son of man is delivered into the hands of men, and they shall kill him; and after that he is killed, he shall rise the third day. But they understood not that saying, and were afraid to ask him." - Mark 9:31-32

"He is not here, but is risen: remember how he spake unto you when he was yet in Galilee, Saying, The Son of man must be delivered into the hands of sinful men, and be crucified, and the third day rise again. And they remembered his words." - Luke 24:6-8

"For we have not an high priest which cannot be touched with the feeling of our infirmities; but was in all points tempted like as we are, yet without sin. Let us therefore come boldly unto the throne of grace, that we may obtain mercy, and find grace to help in time of need."
- Hebrews 4:15-16

Scripture Reading: Matthew 26:36-46

My six-year old can't keep a secret to save his life. If birthday gifts, Christmas presents and other surprises are any indication, I will never be able to count on this kid to cover for me. Oh, he loves his mama, but sometimes his mouth runneth over, and more than once, I've cringed at the details that he has shared with others on my behalf.

But the truth of life is this: *secrets are hard*. In the context of a six-year old, secrets are silly, incoherent whispers, but in the context of adults, secrets are often burdens, heartaches, wounds that never fully heal, and the private agony of wounds yet to come.

In Matthew 26, Jesus knew those kind of secrets. He had tried to share them with His disciples, but their minds could not comprehend, their hearts could not bear the truth, and their bodies were longing for sleep (Verses 36-46). In the weeks leading up to His crucifixion, Jesus had talked about His death, burial, and resurrection (Mark 8:31-34, 9:30-32, John 16:17), but the disciples had somehow blocked it out, clinging to hopes of overthrowing the Romans and arguing over their order of importance in the kingdom to come (Mark 9:33-35).

Only Jesus understood that the hosannas would turn to hatred (John 12:12-16). Only Jesus knew why Judas slipped out of the last supper (John 13:26-30). Only Jesus knew that His kingdom could not be ushered in without a cross (Hebrews 9:22). And only Jesus knew the pain that He really bore on that cross.

I'm not talking about the pain of nails and thorns and multiple beatings, because as horribly excruciating as that was, it wasn't the worst of it. I'm talking about the pain of separation from God, the pain of knowingly bearing every vile and revolting sin ever committed, reliving the sting of every mistake ever made, visiting every dark corner of every dark heart that ever did or ever would beat on this earth - including yours and mine. That was the private agony of Jesus (II Corinthians 5:21, Philippians 2:8, Hebrews 12:2).

But praise God that for three long days, while the disciples hid, and the women wept, and Satan celebrated, and soldiers guarded a grave that they never really had the power to seal, only Jesus knew that it *wasn't* over. Only Jesus knew that He had not died in vain. Only Jesus knew that death was about to meet its own end, and the power of sin was about to be cancelled (I Corinthians 15:54-55).

Sometimes there's great pain in the knowing. Sometimes we carry secrets and burdens to cover ourselves. Sometimes we do it to spare others, and the weight of such burdens can feel impossible to bear - and in truth, it is. But there is a Savior to bear those burdens with you (Psalm 42:5, 46:1, 57:1-3, Philippians 4:6-7). There is a Savior who knows the crushing weight of a truth that others can't begin to wrap their heads around.

And because of that Savior, there is freedom in the knowing and freedom in knowing Him - freedom from sin, freedom from the burden of bearing everything alone, freedom from the feeling that no one will ever understand - because He *does* understand.

As you contemplate Christ's death on the cross and His resurrection from the grave, let me encourage you to find comfort in the knowing, to even rejoice in the knowing. If you bear a pain too great to share with others, tell it to Jesus. He has been there, He has already seen it, and whatever it is, for your sake, He died and rose again to overcome it (Hebrews 10:19-23, 13:5-6, I Peter 1:3-4, 5:6-7) .

Today, regardless of any heartache I have known, I rejoice in knowing this. He is **alive**. He is my **Savior**. He is my **hope**. And He **understands**. **Jesus loves me. THIS I KNOW**.

YOUR PRESCRIPTION

Rejoice in knowing that Christ has conquered sin, death, and everything that has ever hurt you. Take all of your burdens - your secret fears, shame, and heartaches - to Him. He knows them and He longs for you to know victory.

SELF EXAMINATION
Is God speaking to you about a problem with your heart?

_____

_____

_____

_____

_____

TREATMENT PLAN
What steps do you need to take to address your heart problem?

_____

_____

_____

_____

_____

Poster Girls

"And the blood shall be to you for a token upon the houses where ye are: and when I see the blood, I will pass over you, and the plague shall not be upon you to destroy you, when I smite the land of Egypt." - Exodus 12:13

"Behold, when we come into the land, thou shalt bind this line of scarlet thread in the window which thou didst let us down by: and thou shalt bring thy father, and thy mother, and thy brethren, and all thy father's household, home unto thee." - Joshua 2:18

"And Joshua saved Rahab the harlot alive, and her father's household, and all that she had; and she dwelleth in Israel even unto this day; because she hid the messengers, which Joshua sent to spy out Jericho." - Joshua 6:25

Scripture Reading: Joshua 2

I lead a small women's counseling group at my church as part of a faith-based recovery and discipleship program. The program is often underestimated as one that deals solely with addictions, but my years of involvement have shown me that people are there for everything under the sun. Marital problems, hard-to-raise kids, depression, abusive relationships, and eating disorders are just a few of the needs represented.

As we go around the table sharing our personal struggles, I sometimes wonder what I need to talk about. Life is good. God is good, and my problems are few. And yet, when my turn comes, something shameful always spills out. It never takes me long to dredge up my inner rebellion, some regrettable attitude, or some resentment or relapse from the depths of this imperfect woman's heart.

Maybe that's why I love Rahab. She's the poster girl for real women like me.

In Joshua 2, Rahab is one of the most notorious residents of a notorious city - Jericho. She is a harlot, and word reaches the king that two Israelite spies are trying to blend in at the brothel (Verses 1-4).

But while you can question Rahab's morals, you can't question her intelligence. This girl has the fear of the Lord in her (Proverbs 2:5, 9:10, 10:27, 29:25, Isaiah 33:6, Revelation 15:4). She's heard the stories of the Red Sea and Israel's other miraculous victories. She knows that all of Jericho is running scared, and this harlot is ready to put her fate in the hands of the One True God (Joshua 2:9-13, James 2:25).

When questioned about her recent visitors, Rahab sends the king's men on a wild goose chase, telling them that the spies have already left the city. She then hides the spies on the roof of her house and offers them a different kind of proposition - she will save them now, if they will save her later. A deal is struck, and a scarlet cord serves as a way of escape for the spies and a signal of salvation for Rahab and her family.

Rahab's redemption is actually a special foreshadowing of ours. The scarlet cord hung in her window is a sort of Gentile passover, a representation of how Christ would one day bring salvation to you and me. Just as the Jews sprinkled blood on their doorposts in Exodus 12, so that the Angel of Death would pass over their families, Rahab's scarlet cord protected her family from the swords of the Israelite army (Exodus 12, Joshua 2:18-21, 6:17, 22-25, Hebrews 13:12-13).

And by God's grace, Rahab would become a permanent fixture in Israel, eventually marrying into the house of Judah, giving birth to Boaz (the husband of Ruth and great grandfather of David), and finding her own place of grace in the genealogy of Christ (I Chronicles 2:11-12, Ruth 4:20-21, Matthew 1:5, Luke 3:32).

I love Rahab, but more than that, I love the God Who *redeemed* Rahab. Her life was a mess, punctuated by immorality of biblical proportions. But she was not beyond grace, not beyond saving. And she wasn't just rescued, she was restored. All it took was a little healthy fear of a holy God (Psalm 20:6, 33:21, 42:1-2, Habakkuk 2:20, Hebrews 10:31, 11:31, Revelation 4:8).

Today, you and I live in Jericho, where sin and fear run rampant, and few people understand that redemption only comes in the color red - through the shed blood of Jesus Christ (Ephesians 2:13, Hebrews 9:22, I John 1:7). But you and I can know restoration. We can leave our personal Jericho behind, and we can find our place in the plan of God (Jeremiah 29:11, Ephesians 2:8-10).

Take a page out of the story of our poster girl, Rahab, and start with a healthy fear of a holy God. Like our notorious girlfriend, we can go from being casualties of war to poster girls for grace. And with that grace, we can grow to be *more* than conquerors and *all* that God has planned (Romans 8:37-39).

YOUR PRESCRIPTION

Be a poster girl for grace. Take your whole mess to God, and let Him rescue and restore you through the power of His blood. Seek accountability and a place of grace where you can be honest about your struggles and be encouraged in the Lord.

SELF EXAMINATION
Is God speaking to you about a problem with your heart?

_____

_____

_____

_____

_____

TREATMENT PLAN
What steps do you need to take to address your heart problem?

_____

_____

_____

_____

_____

Drama & The Divine

"And Aaron took as Moses commanded, and ran into the midst of the congregation; and, behold, the plague was begun among the people: and he put on incense, and made an atonement for the people. And he stood between the dead and the living; and the plague was stayed."
- Numbers 16:47-48

"All the ways of a man are clean in his own eyes; but the Lord weigheth the spirits."
- Proverbs 16:2

"...Blessed be the name of God for ever and ever: for wisdom and might are his: And he changeth the times and the seasons: he removeth kings, and setteth up kings: he giveth wisdom unto the wise, and knowledge to them that know understanding." - Daniel 2:20b-21

Scripture Reading: Numbers 16

Sometimes I think I should just have my mouth sewn shut. While it may not allow me to learn the much-needed lessons of patience, trust, and humility, at least it would keep me from repeatedly inserting my foot into said mouth.

Situations have been swirling around me lately. In my mind, they beg for a response. In my heart, I know that they're not mine to handle. And yet, it's so easy to get caught up in the drama and lose sight of the Divine. God is working in these situations, and although I *think* I know what needs to be accomplished, He knows what will accomplish His will. And He alone is sovereign.

In Numbers 16, drama was everywhere - the sort of manufactured drama that is the product of people demanding their own way. Moses and Aaron had thankless jobs to be sure, and they now faced opposition from an overly-ambitious Levite named Korah. A Kohathite, Korah belonged to the family of Levites that transported the Ark of the Covenant and managed the setup and takedown of the Tabernacle. They were privileged, but they were not priests, and for Korah, it wasn't enough. In short, Korah wanted Aaron's job, maybe even Moses job, and he had 250 princes of Israel behind him (Verses 1-3, Jude 4, 10-11).

Moses met Korah's challenge with a challenge of his own. They would each offer incense to the Lord, and **God** would decide which was acceptable to Him (Verses 15-19). Of course, God's mind had been made up long before Korah came on the scene. He had hand-picked Moses and Aaron, and Korah was in no position to second-guess the will of God.

Some tense moments follow, as Korah's co-conspirators, Dathan and Abiram, defy Moses, and Moses and Aaron plead with God to spare as many people as possible, in spite of Korah's blatant offense (Verses 12-14, 20-22).

The contest commences, and at Moses' word, everyone lights their incense. But no sooner does Moses finish speaking before the ground splits open, swallowing Korah, his cohorts, their families, and all of their stuff. The earth closes again, and any doubt about who God has chosen is erased (Verses 31-34). Fire and plague follow, and nearly 15,000 are dead by day's end (Verses 42-50).

There's a very telling epilogue to the story of Korah.

Although God resoundingly defended the authority of Moses and Aaron in the wake of Korah's rebellion, the unmistakable humanity of Moses and Aaron would be highlighted in the chapters to come. By Numbers 20 (Verses 1-12), both are denied entrance to the Promised Land after Moses strikes the rock, instead of following God's clear instructions. In essence, the men who had pleaded with God to have patience with His people ultimately lost their own patience and misrepresented the Lord.

Did this vindicate Korah in his rebellion against Moses and Aaron? *Absolutely not.* And here's why: the issue was never the worthiness of Moses and Aaron. They were just men - but regardless of their own choices, they were *God's* choice, *His* chosen men (Daniel 2:20-21, II Chronicles 6:6, Psalm 89:2-4, Isaiah 41:8-9, John 15:16).

The issue was God's sovereignty - His inalienable right as Creator, Lord, and King of Kings to set up whomever He chooses, however He chooses, and to deny us explanation when He so chooses (Psalm 115:3, Proverbs 16:9, I Chronicles 29:11-12, II Chronicles 20:6, Isaiah 46:9-10, Ephesians 1:1).

I'll say it again. **Sometimes we get so wrapped up in drama that it distracts us from the Divine.** And we can be so determined to have our way that we refuse to let God have His way in us (Psalm 139:23-24). Sometimes we're so intent on being right that we simply refuse to submit to God's rule (Psalm 19:12-13).

Sometimes we need to get off our soapbox and get on our knees. Sometimes we need to stop trying to win and realize what we really stand to lose. And in the end, we need to let go, let God, and, let Him **BE** God (Psalm 46:10).

YOUR PRESCRIPTION

Are you struggling to accept God's sovereignty in a specific situation? Do you find yourself refusing to surrender and fighting a battle that isn't yours to fight? Acknowledge God as the Authority in that situation and ask Him to help you to trust His plan.

SELF EXAMINATION
Is God speaking to you about a problem with your heart?

_____

_____

_____

_____

_____

TREATMENT PLAN
What steps do you need to take to address your heart problem?

_____

_____

_____

_____

_____

Take A Seat

"Now it came to pass, as they went, that he entered into a certain village: and a certain woman named Martha received him into her house. And she had a sister called Mary, which also sat at Jesus' feet, and heard his word."
- Luke 10:38-39

"That Christ may dwell in your hearts by faith; that ye, being rooted and grounded in love, May be able to comprehend with all saints what is the breadth, and length, and depth, and height; And to know the love of Christ, which passeth knowledge, that ye might be filled with all the fulness of God." - Ephesians 3:17-19

"Study to shew thyself approved unto God, a workman that needeth not to be ashamed, rightly dividing the word of truth." - II Timothy 2:15

Scripture Reading: Luke 10:38-42; John 12:1-8

I have a confession to make - sometimes I steal stuff from my pastor. Being a pastor's daughter, I know that's actually considered a compliment. And if nothing else, this shows that

I was doing more than planning lunch or anticipating my next cup of coffee during Sunday morning service (though I could always go for a good cup of coffee).

The jumping off point is the story of Mary and Martha in Luke 10:38-42. Of course, this story has been done to death, but it's no wonder, as these five little verses are packed with thought-provoking details.

My pastor recently emphasized that there was more to Martha than meets the eye. She wasn't the villain of the story. She opened her home to the Lord, served, and wanted everything to be right - all good qualities, when kept in proportion to what was "needful". Martha's attitudes and priorities might have needed some tweaking (and she should maybe not assume what Jesus should do on her behalf), but she was a "good girl" who loved the Lord.

But it got me thinking. What really set Martha off? Was it just the work - the extra load of dishes or the fact that the food would be cold by the time it all got on the table? Or was there something more, something that wouldn't necessarily jump off the page to us today?

Mary *"sat at Jesus' feet"*, a term used to describe the process of rabbinical teaching (Deuteronomy 33:3, Luke 8:35, 38-39, 10:39, Acts 22:3). Remember, Jesus was considered to be a teacher by His contemporaries, and He was frequently referred to as "Rabbi". So here's how a Rabbi taught. It was not a one-sided affair. It was an ongoing exchange, where students learned by asking questions, like when the boy Jesus sat with the "doctors" in the temple (Luke 2:42-52). The Bible tells us that young Jesus was listening and "asking them questions".

Can I tell you I think Mary was doing the same thing? Until recently, I've always thought of Mary as a passive listener, someone who sat quietly on the floor, staring wide-eyed at Jesus. My opinion has changed dramatically. I now think that Mary was actively engaged in *discussion* with Jesus - questioning, challenging, determined to understand. It was bold and audacious for a woman of that day, and because her heart longed to know God, her audacity was honored by God.

And I wonder if Martha's impertinence ("Lord, dost thou not care?") and her appalled reaction was really the call of culture. After all, who did Mary think she was? Had she forgotten that her place was in the *kitchen*, and not in the *conversation*? The study of scripture and the opportunity to engage in a dialogue about the ways of God was a privilege reserved for the men of that day. In Jewish culture, access to God began with men, and at best, trickled down to women.

But Jesus challenged Jewish culture and offered everyone - the poor, lepers, publicans and prostitutes, Gentiles, and yes, "good girls" in general - direct access to God, and He died to give us the privilege of reconciliation and a personal relationship with God. (Romans 5:10, Colossians 1:21, I John 3:1)

Mary's audacity had a purpose. In John 12, Mary would anoint Jesus' feet, and Jesus would acknowledge that she was the only one who had really been paying attention (Verses 1-8). Martha still served (Verse 2), but she no longer questioned her sister's place at the feet of Jesus.

And don't you question *your* place, either. No matter where you are in your walk or what your struggles may be, God wants to reveal His heart to you. He wants to give you understanding (Psalm 1:1-3, 90:12, 119:103-104, Proverbs 22:17-18, Jeremiah 33:3, John 16:13-14, Philippians 3:8). His Word is a treasure trove of truth, and He wants you to dig it out, talk it out, and work it out with fear and trembling (Philippians 2:12).

Serve the Lord with gladness, but come before His presence and get to know Him, because He is good, and He deserves our full and audacious attention (Psalm 100). Take a seat at His feet, my friend. We have much to talk about.

YOUR PRESCRIPTION

Study the scriptures for yourself. Ask questions. Pray about them. Take them to your pastor and other Christians. The truths God wants to reveal to us are endless. Never stop learning about Him.

SELF EXAMINATION
Is God speaking to you about a problem with your heart?

_____

_____

_____

_____

_____

TREATMENT PLAN
What steps do you need to take to address your heart problem?

_____

_____

_____

_____

_____

The Urgent & The Important

"And he answered, Fear not: for they that be with us are more than they that be with them. And Elisha prayed, and said, Lord, I pray thee, open his eyes, that he may see. And the Lord opened the eyes of the young man; and he saw: and, behold, the mountain was full of horses and chariots of fire round about Elisha."
- II Chronicles 6:16-17

"Thou hast beset me behind and before, and laid thine hand upon me. Such knowledge is too wonderful for me; it is high, I cannot attain unto it." - Psalm 139:5-6

"For we wrestle not against flesh and blood, but against principalities, against powers, against the rulers of the darkness of this world, against spiritual wickedness in high places. Wherefore take unto you the whole armour of God, that ye may be able to withstand in the evil day, and having done all, to stand." - Ephesians 6:12-13

Scripture Reading: II Kings 6:1-22

Lately, I've been feeling like the rope in a tug of war. One end is being pulled by the *Urgent* - the frenzy of life that is constantly screaming for my attention, telling me to move faster, get this done, and get everything (and I mean, *everything*) under my control. At the other end is the *Important* - the moment-by-moment devotion of the heart that God desires from me, so that He can equip me to face the urgent in a way that glorifies Him.

Because, here's the thing - while everything on the urgent end seems to desperately need *me* (in my mind, anyway), *I* truly and desperately need the Important. And more than once, I have fallen flat on my face in the mud, while trying to tackle the urgent, without the prayer-fueled power of the Important.

II Kings 6 starts with a story of the urgent, followed by a miraculous unveiling of the Important. In the first seven verses, Elisha is urged by the "sons of the prophets" (his apprentices) to help build a larger meeting place for them. In their minds, it's an urgent matter. They proceed to the Jordan River to gather building materials, and in the process, an axe head literally flies off the handle and into the water. To complicate matters, this critical piece of equipment (no doubt the multi-tool of its day) was borrowed.

But don't miss this: **God cares.** We often ignore God in the urgent, because we assume that these problems are just the right size for us to handle - and too small for Him. That is never the case. Elisha steps up, and God does the impossible, causing the iron axe head to float to the surface for retrieval.

Next, the urgency is taken up several notches, as the king of Syria declares war on Elisha (Verses 8-14). The Syrian army had set a trap for the king of Israel, pitching their tents in a strategic location with the intent of ambushing the king. But being a prophet with a direct line to God, Elisha reveals the position of the Syrian army to the king of Israel, and their plan is thwarted.

Realizing that the prophet is the problem, the Syrians surround the city of Dothan and Elisha's home (Verses 15-22). This situation is definitely urgent. Elisha's servant goes into a panic, but the prophet prays. The incredible thing is - Elisha doesn't ask God for help. Instead, He asks God to open the servant's eyes to see the Help that is *already there*. And then we get a glimpse of the battle-ready Divine, as the servant clearly sees an angelic army (complete with chariots of fire) poised to fight on their behalf. The Syrian army is struck blind, and Elisha leads them right into the hands of the army of Israel.

Our enemy is constantly trying to turn our attention away from God, constantly distracting us with the urgent, panicking us into charging ahead without God. But make no mistake about it - God IS the Important - His Word, His presence, His power, and the things that have eternal value in His economy.

And here's what prayer is - prayer is your battle cry against all things urgent, big or small. Prayer tells the forces of heaven to charge on your behalf (I Samuel 17:47, II Chronicles 20:15, Psalm 91:10-12, Daniel 10:18-19). But too often, we tell heaven to stand down. We charge headlong into battles that are not ours to fight, and we leave the source of our power - the power of prayer - behind (Luke 10:19, I Corinthians 15:57, II Corinthians 10:3-4, James 4:2).

What's in front of you may seem urgent and insurmountable, but behind you is the Host of Heaven. You are surrounded by grace, reinforced by the power of the Almighty, and poised for victory - you just need the eyes of Elisha to see the army that is waiting to fight for you (Exodus 14:13-14, II Samuel 22:3-4, Isaiah 54:17, I John 5:14, Matthew 17:20, I John 4:4).

Before you go to battle today, turn your attention to the Important. Prepare your heart, prioritize your thoughts, and pray for eyes to see the *real* conflict. Your All-Important,

All-Sovereign, and Almighty Father will lead the charge on your behalf - because *you* are important to *Him*.

YOUR PRESCRIPTION

Ask God to help you separate the urgent from the important, and ask Him to help you to bring every battle to Him. Get on your knees, and sound your battle cry, knowing God will fight for you.

SELF EXAMINATION
Is God speaking to you about a problem with your heart?

_____

_____

_____

_____

_____

TREATMENT PLAN
What steps do you need to take to address your heart problem?

_____

_____

_____

_____

_____

The Hand-Off

"And they that know thy name will put their trust in thee: for thou, Lord, hast not forsaken them that seek thee." - Psalm 9:10

"Oh how great is thy goodness, which thou hast laid up for them that fear thee; which thou hast wrought for them that trust in thee before the sons of men!" - Psalm 31:19

"Trust in the Lord with all thine heart; and lean not unto thine own understanding. In all thy ways acknowledge him, and he shall direct thy paths." - Proverbs 3:5-6

"And now, brethren, I commend you to God, and to the word of his grace, which is able to build you up, and to give you an inheritance among all them which are sanctified." - Acts 20:32

Scripture Reading: Acts 20:16-38

Watching my husband climb a 20-foot ladder leaned against a 60-foot tree that he's decided to cut down single-handedly. Watching our high-school senior weigh his post-graduation options and negotiate his post-graduation boundaries. Watching our kindergartner boldly ride his bike up the street to the fire hydrant (*his* designated boundary) and back to the distant safety of our driveway.

There's a common thread that runs through all of these images. And that thread is my utter lack of control. It makes my heart rate speed up. It causes me to hyperventilate a little. And it forces me to realize that for all of my desperate attempts at control, I am desperately dependent on my sovereign God.

Maybe that's why I can feel Paul's pain in Acts 20. He is on his way to Jerusalem, hoping to make it in time for Pentecost, but knowing that his many enemies will be waiting for him. He is very intentional on this trip, knowing that persecution, imprisonment, and the possibility of martyrdom always loom over him. And though time won't allow for a stop in Ephesus, he sends for the elders of the Ephesian church and meets with them in Miletus (Verses 16-17).

When the elders arrive, Paul recounts his history with the church at Ephesus, leading into the hand-off of this congregation that is near and dear to his heart. Paul has poured himself into this church, teaching from house to house, spending three years of his ministry building up this church as a humble servant-leader (Verses 18-21, 31), and leaving his adopted son and protege, Timothy, to continue the work there. He has taught them everything he knows about Jesus, the scriptures, salvation, and godly living, preaching the "whole counsel" of God (Verses 27-28, Ephesians 4:11-12, Colossians 3:16, II Timothy 2:2, 3:16, 4:2, Hebrews 13:7).

But for all that Paul has done to shore up this congregation, he knows that they can still be vulnerable to false teachers, their own pride, and all the perversions that still threaten our churches today (Verse 29-31, Matthew 7:15, II Timothy 4:3-4, I John 4:1). And so, he does one final hand-off - the hand-off that you and I need to make over and over in our own lives - and He commends this church to God (Verse 32, Deuteronomy 4:39,

I Chronicles 29:11-12, Psalm 31:19, 37:5, Proverbs 15:3, Isaiah 43:13, 46:10, Hebrews 13:6). With prayers and tears, he leaves another one of his pet projects behind and trusts its unknown future to the God he knows.

I believe that God has entrusted *territory* (I Chronicles 4:10), *talents* (Romans 12:5-7), and *trainees* (Titus 2:3-4) to me in this life. But make no mistake, it is God Who gives the increase, God Who determines the seasons of my service, and God Who decides the outcome of every opportunity. And that's where I often find myself wrestling with the hand-off. And when I do, an immediate heart check is in order (Psalm 139:23-24).

As I sat with a friend this morning, I made a disturbing confession over coffee. I recently read one of my Heart Medicine devotionals from days gone by, only to realize that I wasn't taking any of my own advice. The Lord had given me truths from His Word about changing priorities, changing seasons, and control issues, and I wasn't following any of them. I always admit that every devotional starts with God speaking to me about the things I need to change. What I don't always admit is that I can be the most stubborn and unyielding among us.

So today, I'm ending the *stand-off* and re-instituting the *hand-off*. I'm putting my pride, my preconceived notions, and my pet projects aside, and I'm trusting the future to God. I'm not just depending on sovereignty - I'm delighting in it and looking forward to seeing God do more than I ever could on my own (Ephesians 3:20). And I'm handing off all that I hold dear - to the God that holds me.

YOUR PRESCRIPTION

Are you handing off everything to God? Are you trusting His power and His sovereignty in every area of your life? Ask God to show you the things that you still need to entrust to Him. He is faithful, and He is worthy of your trust in all things.

SELF EXAMINATION
Is God speaking to you about a problem with your heart?

_____

_____

_____

_____

_____

TREATMENT PLAN
What steps do you need to take to address your heart problem?

_____

_____

_____

_____

_____

While He Waits

"For thus saith the Lord God, the Holy One of Israel; In returning and rest shall ye be saved; in quietness and in confidence shall be your strength: and ye would not... And therefore will the Lord wait, that he may be gracious unto you, and therefore will he be exalted, that he may have mercy upon you: for the Lord is a God of judgment: blessed are all they that wait for him."
- Isaiah 30:15, 18

"O Jerusalem, Jerusalem, thou that killest the prophets, and stonest them which are sent unto thee, how often would I have gathered thy children together, even as a hen gathereth her chickens under her wings, and ye would not!"
- Matthew 23:37

"As many as I love, I rebuke and chasten: be zealous therefore, and repent. Behold, I stand at the door, and knock: if any man hear my voice, and open the door, I will come in to him, and will sup with him, and he with me."
- Revelation 3:19-20

Scripture Reading: Isaiah 30

We are in the midst of two graduations at my house - we have both a senior and a kindergartner preparing for the next phase in their young lives. And although they are 13 years apart, my crazy but kind-hearted boys are so much alike - eager, fearless, "wise in their own eyes", and incredibly stubborn. And so this mama prays. Because, especially with the senior, there is way too much that is beyond my control. And when I can see the potential danger, but not the outcome - my utter helplessness humbles me. And so I pray.

You see, even though I'm on the dark side of 45, I remember being where he is right now. I remember the choices I made, the prices I paid, and the lessons learned the hard way. I remember saying that I was "impatient with life" and living like it was entirely up to me to carve out my own destiny. And in the carving, I dug holes that only God could get me out of.

In Isaiah 30, the prophet is trying to warn the kingdom of Judah about the price of impatience. Isaiah prophesied during the reign of King Hezekiah in Jerusalem (II Kings 16-20). At that point in Judah's history, Assyria, led by the ruthless King Sennacherib, was their greatest threat. A few generations earlier, Assyria had captured the Northern Kingdom of Israel, devastating their land and exiling their people. Now the Assyrians threatened the Southern Kingdom of Judah, and Judah prepared to enlist the help of an old enemy, rather than wait on the deliverance of God.

Conveniently forgetting the bondage of their forefathers and the clear commands of God, Jewish envoys traveled to Egypt to negotiate an alliance with the very country that kept them as slaves in the days of Moses. And God's Word is clear - this treaty will be worthless (Verses 2-3, 7). Egypt will not be able to save Judah.

In Verse 6, God's people are going to great lengths to buy the world's protection, sending a caravan of donkeys and camels loaded down with the riches that God Himself had given them. How ironic that they take the blessings of God and use them to try to strike a better deal with the world. And how often do we take God's gracious gifts and gamble them in the world, trading the eternal for the immediate?

Verse 15 sums up the simplicity of God's requirements - *return and rest.* That was all they had to do to find deliverance. God wanted *repentance* - returning to Him - and *trust* - resting in His promises and waiting on His fulfillment of them (Psalm 18:30, 20:7, 37:3, 5, 40, II Chronicles 7:14, Jeremiah 39:18). Sadly, the verse ends with the verdict of their free will - "ye would not."

But don't miss the precious, promised longsuffering of our "Abba" Father (Romans 8:14, Galatians 4:6). In Verse 18, God commits to do the waiting that His people would not. He will wait for them to come to the end of themselves (Luke 15:17-18). He will wait for them to learn their lesson the hard way, and He will wait for them to accept His mercy. God's grace will overcome, but it could have been so much better, so much easier, if they had chosen to wait, instead of leaving the waiting to God (Psalm 31:19, Isaiah 63:7, John 10:10, Romans 2:4).

There have been times in my life when God was waiting on me - waiting to bless me, to use me, to grow me. And in my arrogance, I kept *Him* waiting - always to my own detriment. God has been gracious, and I am blessed, but I forfeited years of His goodness by refusing to wait and trust.

If someone needs to wait - let it be you and me. Wait on God's best. Prove the plans that seem good to you through patient prayer, and rest in the God Who never makes a promise that He will not keep. God longs to be gracious to you. He longs to work in you and through you. The question is: How long will He have to wait on you?

YOUR PRESCRIPTION

Is God waiting on you? Are you so busy controlling your situation that there's no room for God to work in it? Ask Him to show you the things that He wants to accomplish in your situation and in YOU. Surrender to His will and His work in your life.

SELF EXAMINATION
Is God speaking to you about a problem with your heart?

_____

_____

_____

_____

_____

TREATMENT PLAN
What steps do you need to take to address your heart problem?

_____

_____

_____

_____

_____

Beyond the Bad

"And the Lord said, I have surely seen the affliction of my people which are in Egypt, and have heard their cry by reason of their taskmasters; for I know their sorrows; And I am come down to deliver them out of the hand of the Egyptians, and to bring them up out of that land unto a good land and a large..." - Exodus 3:7-8a

"The Lord is my rock, and my fortress, and my deliverer; my God, my strength, in whom I will trust; my buckler, and the horn of my salvation, and my high tower." - Psalm 18:2

"Make us glad according to the days wherein thou hast afflicted us, and the years wherein we have seen evil. Let thy work appear unto thy servants, and thy glory unto their children." - Psalm 90:15-16 (a Psalm of Moses)

Scripture Reading: Exodus 3:1-12, 4:27-31, 5:15-23

I wish I could fix it all. And in my flesh, when someone comes to me desperate and broken, the wheels in my head immediately start turning. What can I say? What can I do? How can I make this better?

And all too often, the truth is - I can't. But I'm learning that deliverance is a journey and a God-ordained process. More than that, deliverance is an ever-growing relationship with God (Psalm 124, Jeremiah 29:13). Because to move beyond the bad - the bondage, the bitterness, the oppression - you have to move towards God. You have to commit to a journey without entirely knowing the destination.

In Exodus 3, God starts a process of deliverance for the Children of Israel. But although God has "come down to deliver them" (Verses 7-8), that deliverance will not come with a simple wave of His sovereign hand.

When God speaks to Moses through the burning bush (Exodus 3:4), He talks of bringing His chosen people to a good land. But it soon becomes clear that victory will not be immediate. Pharaoh's first reaction to Moses', "Let my people go," is to increase the workload of the Israelite slaves (Exodus 5:1, 6-15). Instead of having materials brought to them to make bricks, they will have to gather their own materials, and their quotas will stay the same. In addition, the "officers" (Hebrew supervisors of the workforce) are beaten and blamed for inciting rebellion among the ranks. God's "deliverance" seems devastating.

And even once the plagues begin, they impact the Children of Israel along with the Egyptians. Some Bible scholars believe that the Israelites were not immune to the first three plagues - the Nile turning to blood, the frogs, and the lice. It's not until the fourth plague (flies) that God states that the land of Goshen (home to the Israelite slaves) will not be touched (Exodus 7:14-8:23).

The question is: Why? Why the continued suffering? Why the long, dramatic road out of Egypt?

Let's be real. Pharaoh was no match for God. In His all-powerful, all-knowing sovereignty, God could have wiped Egypt off the map and placed His people in the Promised Land with one word. Pharaoh's cooperation was never a requirement.

But therein lies the proof that God's priority is *relationship*. God didn't have to prove Himself to Pharaoh, to Moses, or to His people. He chose to do so. He chose to show His power, to grow the dependency of His people on Him, and to rekindle His relationship with them in the fire of adversity (Exodus 3:12, Deuteronomy 29:2-4, 29, Romans 5:3-5, 8:17-18, Philippians 3:10, James 1:2-4).

We want quick fixes and immediate answers. And when the pain is intense and life is especially cruel, the desire for fast deliverance is more than understandable. But God wants more for us. He desires the slow, methodical, hand-in-hand process and the day-by-day journey that teaches patience, reveals the truth to us about our own hearts, and finally, replaces our selfish desires with His purpose-filled plans.

It pains me to tell you this, but sometimes, things have to get worse before they can get better.

We pray for deliverance, and we expect God to make all the evil go away, and we can't understand why things seem to continue on their downward spiral, in spite of our prayers. Don't despair. Don't think God hasn't heard. Don't think He hasn't come down to deliver you.

God will show Himself. And rather than simply fixing what is broken on the surface, He will reveal the deep-down brokenness that He wants to heal. He will rebuild the relationships and restore the desolation, and He will redeem it all for His glory (Job 19:25-27, Psalm 90, 106:8, Isaiah 61:3, Zephaniah 3:17, Luke 21:25-29, I Peter 1:7).

By God's grace, you *can* move beyond the bad, but you have to join Him on a journey. Don't worry that you don't know the way, because God does. And use whatever time it takes to take advantage of His presence. He will sustain you. He will show Himself faithful. And one day, He will deliver you to a place beyond the bad.

YOUR PRESCRIPTION

Have you committed to the journey? Pray for deliverance, but while you're waiting on God, get to know God. Prepare to move when He tells you to move, and know that everything - good and bad - can be used by Him to move you beyond the bad.

SELF EXAMINATION
Is God speaking to you about a problem with your heart?

_____

_____

_____

_____

_____

TREATMENT PLAN
What steps do you need to take to address your heart problem?

_____

_____

_____

_____

_____

Who's the Man?

"And David's anger was greatly kindled against the man; and he said to Nathan, As the Lord liveth, the man that hath done this thing shall surely die: And he shall restore the lamb four-fold, because he did this thing, and because he had no pity. And Nathan said to David, Thou art the man." - II Samuel 12:5-7a

"Every way of a man is right in his own eyes: but the Lord pondereth the hearts." - Proverbs 21:2

"Search me, O God, and know my heart: try me, and know my thoughts: And see if there be any wicked way in me, and lead me in the way ever-lasting." - Psalm 139:23-24

"And why beholdest thou the mote that is in thy brother's eye, but considerest not the beam that is in thine own eye? Or how wilt thou say to thy brother, Let me pull out the mote out of thine eye; and, behold, a beam is in thine own eye? Thou hypocrite, first cast out the beam out of thine own eye; and then shalt thou see clearly to cast out the mote out of thy brother's eye."
- Matthew 7:3-5

Scripture Reading: II Samuel 12:1-20

Just when I think I've started to get the worst of me under control, it all comes bubbling to the surface again in spectacular fashion. I'm pushing 50, and for all that time has taken away, it still has not diminished my ability to screw up, to say the wrong thing, to overstep my bounds, or to set myself up for failure.

By God's grace, I'm not what I once was, but I still struggle to admit everything that I actually struggle with. And if anything, I have grown my capacity for self-deception, because somehow, the worst of me still always takes me by surprise.

In II Samuel 12, David is about to come face to face with the worst of himself. Up to this point, he seems to have pulled off the ultimate self-deception. Uriah is long dead, and David's order to murder Uriah on the battlefield is a secret that died with him (II Samuel 11:14-17). Bathsheba is now David's wife, and she's given birth to the son that was conceived while Uriah was away fighting for king and country. What happens at the palace stays at the palace, and David has moved on as if Uriah never existed (II Samuel 11:27). But the last verse of II Samuel 11 tells us that although David has moved on, God is decidedly "displeased", and David's lack of remorse is about to catch up with him.

God sends the prophet Nathan to David, and Nathan begins to tell a story (II Samuel 12:1-4). Nathan's tale about a rich man who heartlessly steals the beloved lamb of a poor man is completely transparent. Still, David is in such denial that he actually believes the rich man to be one of his subjects, and he is prepared to dole out justice and avenge the poor man's loss (Verses 5-6). But David's righteous indignation will soon turn on David himself, as Nathan speaks the awful, long-buried truth (Verse 7), "Thou art the man."

How did it come to this? David was the man after God's own heart, the giant slayer, the sweet psalmist of Israel. Just a few chapters earlier (II Samuel 9), he had reached out to Mephibosheth, the long-lost son of Jonathan, but also the grandson of Saul. He had been kind and gracious, giving the lame and lowly Mephibosheth land, servants, and a permanent seat at the king's table. It was a far different David than the David of II Samuel 11, who got Uriah drunk in the hopes of staging a cover for Bathsheba's ill-conceived pregnancy.

How could the cheating, lying David and the honorable, God-honoring David coexist? Worse still, how could the cheating, lying David be so quick to condemn another?

On any given day, in any given Christian, the flesh and the Holy Spirit are battling for control (Romans 7:15, Colossians 3:9-10, Galatians 5:16, 6:7-8, Ephesians 2:2, 5:1-2, 8-10, II Timothy 2:3-4). The flesh wants to downplay our sin. The flesh looks for easy outs, scapegoats, and bigger sinners and bigger sins that make us feel better about ourselves. But God does not rank sins or sinners - all are equally condemned, and praise God, all are equally redeemed by the blood of Christ (Romans 3:23, 6:23, 8:1).

So who's the man? Sadly, all too often, **I am the man** - the self-deceiving, self-righteous finger-pointer who doesn't realize that he's actually the star character in the prophet's cautionary tale. Are you the man, too? Maybe you've been pointing the finger of denial in someone else's direction. Maybe you've found yourself blaming someone else for the sin that has taken root in your own heart.

My advice to us both - stop hiding behind someone else's sin. Wake up to the truth that God has been waiting for you to confess. **Be the man.** Own your sin, and then give it to God (Psalm 119:80, Jeremiah 17:9, Ezekiel 36:26-27, Hebrews 4:12, I John 1:9). There is forgiveness. There is a better way to move on. And there is redemption in being the man.

YOUR PRESCRIPTION

Are you "the man"? Ask God to show you any sin that you might be harboring in your heart. Stop looking for others to blame, and own the sins that belong to you. Confession really is good for the soul.

SELF EXAMINATION
Is God speaking to you about a problem with your heart?

_____

_____

_____

_____

_____

TREATMENT PLAN
What steps do you need to take to address your heart problem?

_____

_____

_____

_____

_____

Women of Substance

"...For all things come of thee, and of thine own have we given thee." - I Chronicles 29:14b

"Give, and it shall be given unto you; good measure, pressed down, and shaken together, and running over, shall men give into your bosom. For with the same measure that ye mete withal it shall be measured to you again." - Luke 6:38

"Every man according as he purposeth in his heart, so let him give; not grudgingly, or of necessity: for God loveth a cheerful giver."
- II Corinthians 9:7

Scripture Reading: Luke 8:1-3; Acts 9:36-42; Acts 16:9-15

I grew up in a humble home, and as the oldest of four kids, I think my station in life taught me a few things. For instance, clothing, toys, furniture, etc., can all be recycled, repurposed, and reused - over and over again. *Use. Repair. Repeat.* That's pretty much the mantra in a family with four kids. Everything from yesterday's leftovers to plastic shopping bags has multiple applications and infinite possibilities.

God's kingdom isn't much different. God is totally into recycling, and He's an undisputed Master at repurposing. And a life of meaning, purpose, and substance is best found by repurposing your God-given substance for God's higher purpose.

Let me give you a few examples of women in the Bible who took what God gave them, and gave it back to Him:

1. **Joanna, Susanna, and Co.** - In Luke 8:1-3, we are introduced to a group of women who have been healed by Jesus and then joined Him on His travels. And the Bible makes it clear that these women had the critical role of providing for Jesus "of their substance". Joanna, in particular, was the wife of Chuza, who managed Herod's household. Joanna was a woman of means, who brought meaning to her own life by supporting the ministry of Jesus. She gave her wealth to sustain a Savior Who didn't even have a place to call home (Luke 9:58), and served as one of God's means of provision for His Son. Joanna was a woman who could have *been* served, but instead chose *to* serve. And by God's grace, she would be one of the women who first discovered the empty tomb (Luke 24:1-10). All the money in the world couldn't buy a more meaningful moment than that.

2. **Dorcas** - In Acts 9:36-42, Peter travels to Joppa and raises a woman from the dead. But in this story, it's the life of Dorcas that stands out. Verse 36 tells us that Dorcas had a reputation for good works and giving - putting both her money and her skills to work for the Lord. When Peter arrives, he is greeted by weeping widows bearing coats - coats made by the very hands of their dear friend. It's a touching tribute to the tangible impact of Dorcas' ministry. This was a woman who saw the needs of others, loved like Jesus, and was much-loved in return. God gives this humble servant

a resurrection story of her own, and a testimony that would bring even more souls to Christ (Verse 42).

3. **Lydia** - In Acts 16:10, Paul has a vision of a Macedonian man who implores him to come to that region. But ironically, once he arrives in the Macedonian capital of Philippi, the women are the first responders to Paul's ministry (Verse 13). Paul meets Lydia - another woman of means, and in fact, a business owner - down by the riverside. She is saved and baptized, along with her entire household. She then puts that household to work for God, as the Philippian church gets its start right in Lydia's living room (Verses 14-15). Paul would later laud this church for its unrivaled faithfulness in supporting his ministry (Philippians 4:10-19).

Do you see the eternal impact that these humble women had? God recycled, redeemed, and restored their lives, and then repurposed their substance for His glory. I want to be a woman of that kind of substance - not a woman who necessarily *has* a lot, but a woman who *does* a lot for the Lord with whatever she has.

Today, I challenge you to take stock of *your* substance - all of the resources God has given you (Deuteronomy 8:18, Proverbs 3:9, 27, I Samuel 2:7, Malachi 3:10, Matthew 6:21, II Corinthians 9:7-8, Hebrews 10:34, James 1:17). And don't just look at the obvious. God may want to use you and your stuff in creative ways that only a Creator could imagine (I know He's done that for me). The question is: *Are you all in?* A woman of true substance surrenders all the substance she has to the God Who gave it to her in the first place.

YOUR PRESCRIPTION

Ask God to show you new and exciting ways that you can use your substance for Him. He gave you what you have for a reason. You just have to find the meaning behind your means.

SELF EXAMINATION
Is God speaking to you about a problem with your heart?

_____

_____

_____

_____

_____

TREATMENT PLAN
What steps do you need to take to address your heart problem?

_____

_____

_____

_____

_____

Rewind & Remember

"And Moses said unto the people, Remember this day, in which ye came out from Egypt, out of the house of bondage; for by strength of hand the Lord brought you out from this place..."
                                        - Exodus 13:3a

"My soul shall be satisfied as with marrow and fatness; and my mouth shall praise thee with joyful lips: When I remember thee upon my bed, and meditate on thee in the night watches. Because thou hast been my help, therefore in the shadow of thy wings will I rejoice."
                                        - Psalm 63:5-7

"I will remember the works of the Lord: surely I will remember thy wonders of old. I will meditate also of all thy work, and talk of thy doings."
                                        - Psalm 77:11-12

Scripture Reading: Psalm 77

I was sitting in two feet of water in a baby pool in my back-yard. A forty-five pound, blonde-haired torpedo was racing at me full-throttle, and I was bracing myself for impact. I seriously questioned myself for agreeing to Joey's request to "catch" him. There's not a lot of margin for error in an inflatable baby pool - not when you're my size anyway. At best, a mini tidal wave of cold water would slam up my nose and then over my head. At worst, I had willingly submitted to an unintentional drop-kick from a 6-year old.

And then it happened. My mind started to rewind to previous summers. First, to summers spent in a cubicle, where fluorescent lighting was a poor substitute for the glistening July sunlight. Then a few years further back, to a time when I longed for marriage and motherhood and thought neither would ever find their way into my broken life. And even further back, when instead of being waist-deep in water from the garden hose, I was waist-deep in a life of sin and thought I would never find my way out. There's no doubt about it - God has been good to me.

In Psalm 77, the psalmist intentionally rewinds his mind. Something is eating at him. We can't be sure what it is, but it's the kind of gut-wrenching trouble that tortures a soul night and day (Verses 2-4). Whatever it is, we can certainly compare it to some of the trials that keep us awake at night - a wayward child, a marriage hanging by a thread, a dreaded diagnosis, an anxious mind, or looming financial disaster.

Questions start to haunt the psalmist (Verses 7-9) - the kind of questions that Satan loves to taunt us with in our darkest hours. *Where is God? Is He done with me? Has He forgotten me or turned against me?* The writer answers those questions with a deliberate rewind of the mind. In Verse 10, he resolves to shift his focus from the problem at hand to the deliverance and blessings of the past. He then commits to do 3 things (Verses 11-12): *to remember what God has done, to meditate on it, and to talk about it.*

That is good stuff, my friend. When we are so deep in trouble that our struggling minds start to question God's intentions, God's character, and God's very love for us, we need to commit to do those 3 things. **1) Rewind the mind.** Find the memories of God's goodness, of His deliverance. **2) Think on the blessings.** Saturate your soul with the memory of what He has done. And then, **3) Talk about them.** Pepper your conversation with praise. Tell anyone who will listen about the good stuff that you've brought to mind so that you are surrounded - internally and externally - with the truth of Who God is (Deuteronomy 32:3-4, Psalm 89:1, 150:2, Hebrews 11:6, Revelation 5:12).

For the psalmist, the memory of God's deliverance went back to the shores of the Red Sea (Verses 15-20), when God parted the waters for His people to pass through on dry ground, before slamming those same waters down on top of Pharaoh's army (Exodus 14). And in Deuteronomy, God commanded the Children of Israel multiple times to remember that very incident, and to trust and obey Him based on that memory (Deuteronomy 5:15, 7:18, 24:18, Psalm 136:13-15).

So what has God done for you? Even if your years have been flooded with pain, you can still find some evidence of God's intervention on your behalf, His protection, and His mercy (Lamentations 3:19-26). And most likely, you have no shortage of stories about the faithfulness and blessing of God.

Whatever you are facing today, let me encourage you to rewind your mind. Fill your head, your heart, and your every interaction with the memories of all that He has done for you. Replace the complaints, the questions, and the worries with your own firsthand knowledge of the God Who still parts the seas, calms the storms, and walks through all of them with us (Deuteronomy 26:8, Joshua 1:5, 4:23, Isaiah 43:2, Zephaniah 3:17, Romans 5:3-5, I Peter 5:10).

Remember what God has done in the past, and rest in the truth that He will do it again.

YOUR PRESCRIPTION

Take the time to note some of the victories that God has given you and find someone to share them with. Publicly praise God for what He's done, and privately trust that He's working again on your behalf.

SELF EXAMINATION
Is God speaking to you about a problem with your heart?

_____

_____

_____

_____

_____

TREATMENT PLAN
What steps do you need to take to address your heart problem?

_____

_____

_____

_____

_____

The Mind of Me

"For the weapons of our warfare are not carnal, but mighty through God to the pulling down of strong holds;) Casting down imaginations, and every high thing that exalteth itself against the knowledge of God, and bringing into captivity every thought to the obedience of Christ."
                                    - II Corinthians 10:4-5

"I beseech Euodias, and beseech Syntyche, that they be of the same mind in the Lord. And I intreat thee also, true yokefellow, help those women which laboured with me in the gospel, with Clement also, and with other my fellowlabourers, whose names are in the book of life."
                                    - Philippians 4:2-3

"Put on therefore, as the elect of God, holy and beloved, bowels of mercies, kindness, humbleness of mind, meekness, longsuffering; Forbearing one another, and forgiving one another, if any man have a quarrel against any: even as Christ forgave you, so also do ye."
                                    - Colossians 3:12-13

Scripture Reading: Philippians 4

There's something seriously wrong with me. When I explain it to you, you'll think I'm crazy. (And if you didn't already think that, then you just haven't been paying attention.)

Here it is - *sometimes, in my head, I fight with people who have absolutely no idea that I'm fighting with them*. I told you it was crazy. When I put it in writing, it looks so crazy that I'm struggling not to peck at the 'delete' key on my laptop.

There's a downside to being non-confrontational, because the truth is that confrontation is a part of life (Matthew 18:15, Galatians 6:1, James 5:16). And I'm learning that avoiding confrontation doesn't eliminate the problem. Actually, the avoidance just internalizes it.

In Philippians 4, Paul confronts a problem (or should I say 'two problems') head on. He calls out, by name, two of the women in the Philippian church - Euodias and Syntyche (Verse 2). His direct plea to them is brief, but crystal clear. It reminds me of the sobering line my dad often used when we bickered as kids in the backseat of the station wagon, "Knock it off."

Paul urges these women to knock it off. Whatever issue they have with each other in their minds, that's not the issue to Paul. Because here's the true issue - family fights have no place in the family of God (Romans 12:3, 17-19, Galatians 6:9-10, Ephesians 4:1-3, 22-32, I Peter 2:17).

In this passage, the sobering lines come in Verse 3, when Paul acknowledges that these women were instrumental in the early days of that church. He talks about their work in the church, and the fact that their names were written in the Book of Life.

Euodias and Syntyche weren't fly-by-night Christians. They were committed. Their faith was real and active. And yet, their failure to set aside their differences was enough of a threat to the church that Paul needed to address it in an open letter.

And this is a great church. Paul talks at length about the generosity of the Philippian church and their faithful support of his ministry (Philippians 4:10, 14-17). This was a church where the women had been the first converts and a driving force in the work (Acts 16:13-15).

Paul never gives us the details of the dispute between Euodias and Syntyche, but maybe it's better that way. It gives us the freedom to fill in the blank with our own comparable divides - whether it's something as petty as the color of the carpet or something as significant as sugar-coated sin.

And it's no coincidence that Paul's rebuke is sandwiched between admonitions to run the race and resist a worldly mindset, and reminders to cultivate the mind of Christ through rejoicing, prayer, and thinking on the right things (Philippians 3:13-15, 18-19, 4:5-8).

Somewhere along the way, Euodias and Syntyche had lost their focus on Christ, and they had instead focused on each other. Maybe they competed for position or influence in the church. Maybe one of them had seriously and truly wronged the other. Maybe it was a simple misunderstanding, but regardless of who was right and who was wrong, the glorification of their grudge was stealing glory from God and hurting the cause of Christ - and that alone made them *both* wrong (James 3:14-4:1).

I told you about the secret fights in my head, and the truth is, they are often fueled by an excess of pride, indignation, and self-seeking and a lack of mercy, forgiveness, and compassion. The mind that *fights with people who have absolutely no idea that I'm fighting with them* is **not** the mind of Christ - it is undeniably and most ashamedly the mind of **ME**.

So what's on your mind today? Are you nursing a grudge, growing a root of bitterness, or fighting a fight that should have ended long ago? Today, I'm praying to lose MY mind, because the mind of ME and the mind of Christ just aren't the same. And when I'm in my right mind, I want my mind and my heart to be all His and all for His glory.

YOUR PRESCRIPTION

Lose your mind. Confess any secret fights to God, turn away from them, and humble yourself. Ask God to give you the mind of Christ. Fighting has no place among the faithful, so make it right, or in the words of my dad, "Knock it off."

SELF EXAMINATION
Is God speaking to you about a problem with your heart?

_____

_____

_____

_____

_____

TREATMENT PLAN
What steps do you need to take to address your heart problem?

_____

_____

_____

_____

_____

May God Prevail

"And Jacob was left alone; and there wrestled a man with him until the breaking of the day. And when he saw that he prevailed not against him, he touched the hollow of his thigh; and the hollow of Jacob's thigh was out of joint, as he wrestled with him." - Genesis 23:24-25

"Be still, and know that I am God: I will be exalted among the heathen, I will be exalted in the earth." - Psalm 46:10

"Wherefore, my beloved, as ye have always obeyed, not as in my presence only, but now much more in my absence, work out your own salvation with fear and trembling. For it is God which worketh in you both to will and to do of his good pleasure." - Philippians 2:12-13

Scripture Reading: Genesis 32

My schedule and my closet have a lot in common. Both end up jam-packed, despite my best attempts to sort, simplify, and space-save. Both have the potential to descend into chaos faster than you can say, "Maybe I should move this."

And both are the perfect blend of my desperate need for control and my obvious inability to control anything.

In Genesis 32, Jacob is in the presence of angels, and he's still grasping for control. Fresh from his divine deliverance from his unsavory father-in-law Laban in Chapter 31, Jacob is gearing up for yet another awkward confrontation (this time, with his estranged brother Esau).

But before we get to Esau's arrival, let me tell you what Jacob has seen up to this point. In Genesis 31, God appeared to Jacob (Verse 3) and told him it was time to leave Laban behind and return home, promising to protect him along the way. God did just that, appearing to Laban in a dream and literally putting the fear of God in Him before he caught up to Jacob (Verse 24).

As Laban goes home empty-handed, Jacob is greeted by angels at the beginning of Chapter 32 (could there possibly be more proof that God is on Jacob's side?). And yet, this compulsive conniver whose name means "grabber" is desperately working to control the outcome of his next confrontation.

Jacob sends messengers. He offers gifts (Genesis 32:3-5). He sorts his wives and kids in order of importance to him (more awkwardness), and hedges his bets in every possible way (Genesis 32:22-23, 33:1-2). I imagine the angels looking at each other and saying, "Is this guy for real?"

And as for prayer - Jacob prays, but he ultimately spends way more time plotting, after the first round of messengers returns with reports that Esau has 400 men with him.

And then God steps in again. Divine promises and directional dreams weren't enough. Muzzling Laban wasn't enough. Actually meeting his angelic security detail face-to-face didn't deter Jacob. The "grabber" is still grasping at straws. So now, God grabs a hold of him, and the struggle in Jacob's heart materializes in the form of an actual, physical wrestling match between them.

It's an amazing visual - and a telling one - because for a time, God lets Jacob win. He even tries to talk Jacob into letting go (the perfect picture of our free will meeting God's permissive will), but Jacob can't stop fighting for control. God patiently holds back His true power, until He finally maims Jacob, dislocating his hip, and leaving him with a lifelong reminder of his own fragility.

And the next morning, God pours out more grace on Jacob than he ever could have imagined (Psalm 37:23, Proverbs 16:7, 21:1, Isaiah 1:18, Romans 8:37, Ephesians 3:20). Jacob fears a massacre but finds a marshmallow (Verses 8-11), as he and Esau have a surprisingly sweet and tearful reunion (Genesis 33:4).

Why do we fight for control, when we know deep down that we're not equipped to control anything? Why do we wrestle with a God Who loves us so much that He puts up with our childish resistance and lets us win, even though we never deserve to win?

Jacob thought Esau was the enemy, but the enemy all along was his own stubborn will - his struggle to trust the outcome to God.

In the end, God gives the "grabber" a new name - "Israel". You'll find literal interpretations of the name, such as "he who wrestles" or "he struggles with God". But I love the more proverbial definition, because it speaks to the deep-down cry of my stubborn-but-striving heart - "may God prevail".

Is your hip hurting today? Mine's been bothering me for weeks. And so, my prayer for us is this. May we stop wrestling and start realizing that God is Who He says He Is (Exodus 3:14, Job 42:2, Hebrews 11:6). May we plot less and pray all the more (Proverbs 16:9, Romans 12:12, Ephesians 6:18, I Thessalonians 5:17). May we find that God has already won the battle (I Samuel 17:47), and there really is victory in being still (Psalm 46:1).

And in the end - when we finally stop fighting His perfect plan - *may God prevail.*

YOUR PRESCRIPTION

Admit defeat. Surrender your will to God, and ask Him to help you to trust Him for the outcome in your situation. His will and His way are worth the wait, so be still and let Him prevail.

SELF EXAMINATION
Is God speaking to you about a problem with your heart?

_____

_____

_____

_____

_____

TREATMENT PLAN
What steps do you need to take to address your heart problem?

_____

_____

_____

_____

_____

Call It

"And Caleb stilled the people before Moses, and said, Let us go up at once, and possess it; for we are well able to overcome it. But the men that went up with him said, We be not able to go up against the people; for they are stronger than we." - Numbers 13:30-31

"Death and life are in the power of the tongue: and they that love it shall eat the fruit thereof." - Proverbs 18:21

"For verily I say unto you, That whosoever shall say unto this mountain, Be thou removed, and be thou cast into the sea; and shall not doubt in his heart, but shall believe that those things which he saith shall come to pass; he shall have whatsoever he saith." - Mark 11:23

Scripture Reading: Numbers 13

I have seen God's grace shatter a lot of nevers in recent weeks - from simple, everyday things to desperate, seemingly-impossible prayers. I've had to admit my own faithlessness, my own preconceived notions, and the words like "never", "can't", and "always" that I have stubbornly and shortsightedly willed into fact. And it strikes me that, in matters of faith, we need to choose our words carefully.

In Numbers 13, we see careless, faithless, fear-filled words showcased side by side with words that are well-chosen, fearless, and faith-filled. The Children of Israel are on the outskirts of the Promised Land. They are camped in the wilderness of Paran, and God has given Moses a command - send men to search out the land of Canaan (Verses 1-3). Moses chooses a man to represent each tribe, and the twelve spies embark on a 40-day, fact-finding mission in uncharted territory (Verses 17-25).

In the 20/20 vision of hindsight, we can see that this mission was actually a test. God certainly knew what was in the Promised Land - good and bad - and He had repeatedly promised victory and blessing for His chosen people, in return for obedience and faith (Genesis 12:7, 13:15, 17:8, 50:24, Exodus 6:8, Leviticus 20:24). Now, it was time to see if the Children of Israel could trust and obey when promises and problems collided.

The spies return with the fruit of the land - including a single cluster of grapes so large that two men have to carry it on a pole that extends from one's shoulder to the other's (Verses 23, 26). But this physical, tangible, edible proof of God's abundant promise will soon be overshadowed by the foreshadowing of doom by ten of the spies.

Don't miss the weight of words here. While the ten spies concede that the land is amazing and beyond all expectations, their report (defined as an "evil" report in Verse 32) of giants and fortified cities is laden with heavy words of discouragement, statements of absolute impossibility, and declarations of failure (Verses 28-29, 32-33).

Their pragmatism is prophetic. It sends the masses into such an emotional tailspin that they actually start talking about returning to Egypt, and it guarantees that an entire generation will die in the wilderness without ever seeing the Promised Land (Numbers 14:2-4, 20-24).

Caleb and Joshua speak words of faith and hope (Numbers 13:30, 14:6-9), and they will live to lead the next generation to possess the land (Numbers 14:30-33). But the evil report of the other spies literally keeps the rest of Israel out of the place of blessing, by feeding their fears and starving their already-emaciated faith.

Too often, we take pride in "calling it".

We want to be the pragmatic prophet of doom who saw failure looming on the horizon before anyone else did, and we take some sort of sad satisfaction in predicting evil and then watching it come true (James 5:6-10). We label people and situations with words like "never", "can't", and "always" and then wonder why God's promises don't take root in our lives.

Let me set the record straight - God delights in dreamers (I Chronicles 4:10, II Chronicles 16:9, Proverbs 3:5-6, Nahum 1:7, Matthew 8:10, 15:28, Ephesians 3:20-21). He unleashes His greatest blessings in the lives of the unrealistic - the ones who choose promises over practicality and press forward in hope (Matthew 17:20, 19:26, Luke 1:37, Hebrews 11).

Today, I don't want to be the one who "called it", the one who "saw it coming", or the one who "knew it all along". I want to be the one who spoke faith and hope into a situation and saw God do the impossible. I want to be the one who held on to the promise in the face of the problem and believed that God would make a way.

Call the impossible "possible". Call God true and every man a liar. Fill the hopeless with hope, and feed the fearful with faith. Say that He is able to do it, and He will.

YOUR PRESCRIPTION

Choose your words carefully. Speak hope and blessing to the people and situations in your life - even when the words don't seem to make sense. Trust that God is faithful, and He will do what He has promised.

SELF EXAMINATION
Is God speaking to you about a problem with your heart?

_____

_____

_____

_____

_____

TREATMENT PLAN
What steps do you need to take to address your heart problem?

_____

_____

_____

_____

_____

The Small Stuff

"What is man, that thou art mindful of him? and the son of man, that thou visitest him?"
- Psalm 8:4

"But it is good for me to draw near to God: I have put my trust in the Lord God, that I may declare all thy works." - Psalm 73:28

"O Lord, thou hast searched me, and known me. Thou knowest my downsitting and mine uprising, thou understandest my thought afar off. Thou compassest my path and my lying down, and art acquainted with all my ways." - Psalm 139:1-3

Scripture Reading: Psalm 139

I'll admit it - I'm a cheap date. You'll often find me accompanying my husband to Lowes, Home Depot, and a variety of auto parts stores. I try to look like a regular, but I'm sure I stick out like a sore thumb, and I usually only have the most rudimentary understanding of why we're even there.

And the truth is, I'm just happy to be along for the ride. I love following this guy around who is my polar opposite on the outside, and my true, God-given soulmate on the inside (and he's cute, too). I love seeing his brilliance in all the things I don't understand. And because he understands me, he always grabs a bottle of Coke from the refrigerated drink case at the checkout and presents it to me as we head to the parking lot.

In Psalm 139, David marvels at the God Who understands him, and he articulates the balance of awe and intimacy that God desires from each of us.

I particularly love the lines of Verses 2 and 3, where God is essentially interested, even invested, in our every waking moment. It's a truth that we all too often miss the opportunity to live in - maybe because we assume that a Big God can't be bothered with the small stuff. But consider Verses 13-16, where the Creator of the universe meticulously designs and records every detail of David's life - forming his body and numbering his days.

Throughout the chapter, David refers to the eternal, every-where presence of God, but here's the awesome part - it's not just that God is omnipresent (though that's certainly true), it's the incomprehensible truth that God chooses to be present in every aspect of our lives.

David believed that God cared about every last shred of his existence. More importantly, he understood that God had a specific design for His life that could only be accomplished through even deeper intimacy. And in verses 23-24, David welcomes God's honest opinion of anything that needs to change in his life.

Do we welcome that kind of invasive examination of the heart and motives? And do we even care to see the things that only God can show us in ourselves?

His total knowledge of us is more than just a super power; it's a desire on His part to share His intimate knowledge of us *with* us, so He can further shape us and work in us day in and day out. But while God chooses to care about everything that concerns you, only YOU can choose to involve Him in everything (Psalm 8, 56:8, 116, 121, 138:8, Jeremiah 29:11-13, 33:3, Matthew 6:31-32, Philippians 1:6).

And let me stress this. The more familiar you are with God when life seems calm and quiet, the better-equipped you'll be for the storms. And it's much easier to run to the throne for help, when every moment is already a running conversation with God (Psalm 145:18, Hebrews 4:16, 10:22, James 4:8).

So ask yourself - are there areas of your life that you've simply left God out of? Are there little everyday things that seem to be small enough for you to handle in your own strength? Do you have a hard time believing that a mighty God cares about your silly little problems?

Let me invite you to invite God into the little things. Invite Him along for the ride - not just because you need Him (although you do), but because you want to know Him the way He knows you. Don't marginalize His influence in your life or reduce Him to "in case of emergency" status. True relationship is forged in the sweat of the small stuff - the sharing of everyday experiences, ragged routines, and mundane moments (Psalm 121, Isaiah 43:1-3, 49:16, 54:5, Matthew 11:28-30, Luke 12:7, I Peter 5:6-7).

Share the small stuff with our Big God, and be in awe of the fact that YOU are such a big deal to Him.

YOUR PRESCRIPTION

Where does your day take you? Do you always take God along? Do a little self-examination, and ask God to show you the small stuff that He wants to use to bring you closer to Him.

SELF EXAMINATION
Is God speaking to you about a problem with your heart?

_____

_____

_____

_____

_____

TREATMENT PLAN
What steps do you need to take to address your heart problem?

_____

_____

_____

_____

_____

Hands Folded

"As for me, I will call upon God; and the Lord shall save me. Evening, and morning, and at noon, will I pray, and cry aloud: and he shall hear my voice." - Psalm 55:16-17

"And I set my face unto the Lord God, to seek by prayer and supplications, with fasting, and sackcloth, and ashes...O Lord, hear; O Lord, forgive; O Lord, hearken and do; defer not, for thine own sake, O my God: for thy city and thy people are called by thy name." - Daniel 9:3, 19

"Confess your faults one to another, and pray one for another, that ye may be healed. The effectual fervent prayer of a righteous man availeth much." - James 5:16

Scripture Reading: Daniel 9:1-23

Today, I'm fighting the urge to fidget. There's so much I want to fix - even though my "fixing" would probably only make things worse. My mind goes back to my beloved kindergarten teacher, Mrs. Baun, who would patiently tell her small class of wiggly worms to sit at their desks with hands folded.

It was a time-tested way to bring a room full of fidgeting five-year olds back into line.

As I'm itching to wrap my feeble hands around a few situations in my little corner of the world, I'm reminding myself to sit today with my hands folded once again - this time, in prayer.

In Daniel 9, Daniel himself fights the urge to fidget by folding his hands in prayer. A changing of the guard has taken place in Babylon, and Daniel knows that a critical juncture is approaching. The Babylonian Empire has given way to the Persian Empire, and there's a new sheriff in town. Verse 1 tells us that it is the first year of Darius the Mede, and Daniel continues to hold his coveted, God-given position as deputy.

At this point, the Jews have been captives for more than 65 years, and Daniel knows two things. First of all, God has promised to end their captivity after 70 years (Jeremiah 25:11-13, 29:10). Secondly, God has promised (more than 150 years earlier, in Isaiah 44:28-45:1) to use King Cyrus of Persia to release the Jews from their captivity. Cyrus is now in place, and he has appointed Darius to rule over the province of Babylon.

Frankly, I don't know how Daniel contained himself. Prophecies are colliding with the present (Daniel 9:2). Hope is on the horizon, and as he has been for years, Daniel is well-positioned to influence events around him. And yet, Daniel never makes a power play. He never gets ahead of God. Instead, he gets out his sackcloth, skips breakfast, and prays harder than he ever has before (Verses 3-4).

Somehow, Daniel always chose intercession over interference. By God's grace, he spent his entire adult life in the presence of kings. And while kings came and went, Daniel was consistently ranked as one of the three most powerful people in Babylon (Daniel 2:48, 5:28, 6:1-2), and yet, everything Daniel did was accomplished solely through prayer.

Honestly, I wish I had that kind of restraint (Psalm 5:3, 37:7, Isaiah 30:8, Hosea 12:6, Micah 7:7, Philippians 4:6-7, I Peter 5:6-7). So often, I want to take whatever opportunities or influence God has given me and just run with it. And I'm just prideful enough - and at the same time, dumb enough - to think that my forced outcomes would be best.

And that brings me to an important aspect of Daniel's prayer. It is filled with humble references like, "We have sinned" (Verses 2-11, 15). Daniel doesn't presume that he can't possibly be part of the problem. Daniel prays as if God's plan hinges on the condition of his heart - rather than the conniving of his hands - and he seeks a clean conscience before God and a clean slate for his people (Verses 11-13, Deuteronomy 28, Jeremiah 18:6-10, James 4:7-8).

Here's what Daniel didn't know. Although the story of his famous night in the lion's den is told a few chapters earlier in Daniel 6, in actuality, the lion's den was yet to come (remember, it was King Darius that would be tricked into sending Daniel there). And while God had a comprehensive plan to restore His own people in time, He would use Daniel in the meantime to prove His power to the Persians (Daniel 6:25-28).

If you're at a critical juncture today, let me dare you to be a Daniel. Determine to have a faith-filled refusal to force the outcomes on your own, a humble heart willing to be corrected, and most importantly, a head bowed in prayer - hands folded.

YOUR PRESCRIPTION

Take it to the Lord in prayer. Don't fix it - even if a solution seems within reach. Lay your request before God, ask Him to show you the true intents of your heart, and let Him take the lead in your time of need.

SELF EXAMINATION

Is God speaking to you about a problem with your heart?

_____

_____

_____

_____

_____

TREATMENT PLAN

What steps do you need to take to address your heart problem?

_____

_____

_____

_____

_____

Those Crazy Kids

"Whosoever therefore shall humble himself as this little child, the same is greatest in the kingdom of heaven. And whoso shall receive one such little child in my name receiveth me. But whoso shall offend one of these little ones which believe in me, it were better for him that a millstone were hanged about his neck, and that he were drowned in the depth of the sea."
- Matthew 18:4-6

"Being confident of this very thing, that he which hath begun a good work in you will perform it until the day of Jesus Christ." - Philippians 1:6

"Only Luke is with me. Take Mark, and bring him with thee: for he is profitable to me for the ministry." - II Timothy 4:11

Scripture Reading: Acts 15:36-41

My driveway is an obstacle course. Our nineteen-year old has ramps to lift his Volkswagen off the ground for the endless repairs associated with a car that cost less than a thousand dollars. Our six-year old has ramps for jumping his scooter, his bike, and anything else on wheels that doesn't require a license. And then there are the random objects that seem to be set up for the sheer entertainment of watching me trip over them as I make my way to my car (I've never been known for my gracefulness).

But regardless of the obstacles in our driveway and in life, I love those crazy kids with all my heart, and I'm often comforted by the fact that God loves them even more than I do.

In Acts 15, we meet a crazy kid named Mark (a.k.a. John Mark). Actually, we're introduced briefly to Mark in Acts 12:12, when his mother hosts what may have been Jerusalem's most exciting prayer meeting of all time. Young Mark probably had a front row seat that night, when Peter miraculously showed up at the door as the saints were praying for his release from prison. Perhaps it was that very miracle that prompted this wide-eyed young Christian to join his Uncle Barnabas and the Apostle Paul on their next missionary journey (Acts 12:25). But somewhere between the cities of Paphos and Perga, something went wrong, and Mark hightailed it back to Jerusalem (Acts 13:13).

The Bible doesn't give us many details, but in Acts 15, Mark's failure seems to breed more failure, as the memory of his desertion causes a devastating rift between Barnabas and Paul. Barnabas wants to give his nephew a second chance, but Paul doesn't want to have anything to do with him. Verses 37-39 give us the distinct impression that their disagreement did not end well. Barnabas and Mark go one way, and Paul and his new partner, Silas, go another.

To be honest, Mark doesn't look like a very good bet at this point. Paul's strong reaction implies the worst about Mark's character (or the lack thereof). Barnabas even comes off as a little crazy, over protecting and overindulging his good-for-nothing nephew, but God is not nearly finished with the young man named Mark.

Mark is referenced four more times in the New Testament, and unlike the account in Acts, these references are impeccable

(Colossians 4:10, II Timothy 4:11, Philemon 19, 23-24, I Peter 5:13). He goes on to assist Peter in church planting, before proving himself to Paul, who would mention Mark's faithfulness in three different epistles. Perhaps most notably, Mark would author the gospel that bears his name, serving as scribe to Peter's eyewitness account of the life and ministry of Christ.

For the record, Barnabas wasn't crazy - he was Christ-like. The "son of consolation" was right to treat Mark like a son in spite of his early failings (Proverbs 25:11, Isaiah 35:3-4, Acts 4:36, Galatians 6:1, I Peter 4:8). And in His sovereignty, God used the *falling out* between Paul and Barnabas, as a *calling out* of young Mark (Psalm 138:8, Jeremiah 29:11, Romans 8:28, Ephesians 2:10).

God bless our crazy kids. May we love them through their failures, pray circles around them each day, and carry them to the cross. May we remind them (and ourselves) that God never gives up on them, so that they never give up on God. And may we have enough humility to admit that, outside of the grace of God, we were once crazy kids, too.

Today, this imperfect mom is resting in God's unfailing ability to bring good out of my not-so-good. I trust His unfailing love that covers me, even when I'm not so lovable. And I praise God that, unlike me, He never starts anything He doesn't plan to complete.

My dad always said that as long as we have "breath in our bodies and sense in our heads", God is not finished with us yet. And so, I commit my crazy kids (and their crazy mama) to my sovereign God and His ever-loving, ever-working hands.

YOUR PRESCRIPTION

Commit your kids to the Lord. Pray a hedge of protection around them and pray to be the example that they need. And remember, whether you have kids or not, every Christian can have spiritual sons and daughters, and every Christian can point kids to Christ.

SELF EXAMINATION
Is God speaking to you about a problem with your heart?

_____

_____

_____

_____

_____

TREATMENT PLAN
What steps do you need to take to address your heart problem?

_____

_____

_____

_____

_____

About the Author

B ased in the Rochester, NY area, Greta Brokaw is available to speak at your next women's event or to sing at any church event. To request a CD, or for additional booking information, email heartmedicinebook@gmail.com.

For more information about Heart Medicine Ministries, visit myheartmedicine.com or download the free Heart Medicine Devotions app on the App Store or Google Play.

CPSIA information can be obtained
at www.ICGtesting.com
Printed in the USA
BVHW042129171118
533398BV00020B/276/P